CHRISTMAS REVISITED

Robert Brenner

THIRD EDITION WITH REVISED PRICE GUIDE

Schiffer Publishing Ltd®

4880 Lower Valley Road, Atglen, PA 19310 USA

The value for any object is dependent upon numerous conditions. The values herein are only estimates. Neither the author nor the publishers are responsible for any outcomes resulting from consulting this guide.

Revised price guide: 2004
Copyright © 1986, 1999 & 2004 by Robert Brenner.
Library of Congress Control Number: 2004102486

ISBN: 0-7643-1906-X
Printed in China
1 2 3 4

Published by Schiffer Publishing Ltd.
4880 Lower Valley Road
Atglen, PA 19310
Phone: (610) 593-1777; Fax: (610) 593-2002
E-mail: Info@schifferbooks.com
Please visit our web site catalog at **www.schifferbooks.com**

In Europe, Schiffer books are distributed by Bushwood Books
6 Marksbury Avenue Kew Gardens
Surrey TW9 4JF England
Phone: 44 (0) 20-8392-8585; Fax: 44 (0) 20-8392-9876
E-mail: info@bushwoodbooks.co.uk
Free postage in the UK. Europe: air mail at cost.

This book may be purchased from the publisher.
Include $3.95 for shipping. Please try your bookstore first.
We are always looking for people to write books on new and related subjects.
If you have an idea for a book please contact us at the above address.
You may write for a free catalog.

CONTENTS

ACKNOWLEDGEMENTS

Postcard—Germany 1911. $35-45

A book of this magnitude would not have been possible without the advice, friendship, and help of so many collectors and Christmas historians. Most of all, I owe my gratitude and appreciation to my wife Sharon, who constantly supports all my efforts and helps so diligently with revisions and editing. Once again, Peter Schiffer served as a constant pillar of encouragement and strength in spite of numerous writing obstacles and problems.

Princeton's two very competent librarians, Lorraine Cederholm and Shirley Hamaishi, promptly and courteously filled every historical information request and proved again that small communities such as Princeton have the most professional of staff in their libraries.

A most special thanks must go to Wally Bronner and his immediate staff. Wally generously provided a wealth of information regarding Italian ornaments, as well as a multitude of ornaments for photographic purposes. Though an extremely busy person, he took hours of his precious time to help in the preparation of *Christmas Revisited*.

Three collectors of Christmas memorabilia warrant special thanks. Mary Lou Holt has been of the utmost help through encouragement and her generous sharing of a wealth of information. Her willingness to provide photographic material has been unparalleled in the preparation of this book. Maxime Caldwell also supplied a vast amount of experience and photographic material. Dale Kelly and his "treasure chest" of information on toys was of great help in the preparation of photographs contained in that particular section.

The opening of one's home and collection to an author can be trying and, at times, very time consuming. It is to these individuals who allowed me to photograph their collections that I owe a great deal of gratitude. The following individuals provided Christmas memorabilia for photographic purposes: Lorna Gierach, Jim Large, Ron and Sandi Lemelin, Mary Lou Holt, Maxime Caldwell, Connie Herrall, Ed and Bettie Petzoldt, Marsha Westfall, Dale Kelly, Ruth Ruege, Ken and Fran Abendroth, Wally Bronner, and Doris Reda. These individuals have not been listed in a particular order as each of them was of utmost importance to the photography in *Christmas Revisited*.

There are countless others who have provided text information in various fashions. Thanks go to Lorna Beane, Bob Drake, Jerry Ehernberger, Roberta Fiene, Lorna Gierach, Nada Gray, Lynn Klein, Michael Makurat, Dawayne Nowak, Nancy Rouette, Ruth Ruege, Connie Sherer, Thomas Strickfaden, Todd Wachholz, and Marilyn Zenig.

Close friends have continued to provide love and encouragement. Thank you, Mike, Fred, Lorraine, Florence, and Herb.

DEDICATION

It is to Grandmother Reinl that I dedicate this book. Personally, she thinks little about Christmas collecting, however, she has inspired her children and grandchildren to be celebrators of a Christian Christmas. It is her love and inspiration that has motivated us all.

Postcard—Germany 1914. $45-55

"Santa Claus Is Coming!," by Thomas Worth. From *Harper's Weekly*, Dec. 26, 1874.

Chapter 1

SANTA FIGURES

Whatever you call him—*Santa Claus, Father Christmas, Weihnachtsmann, Pelznickel, or Kris Kringle*—he was the one figure that graced almost every tree and decorated every American home during the Christmas season. If only a few cents were available for the purchase of an ornament, it would be for Santa. If more pennies were available, candy containers, Santa dolls, or numerous Santa related items would be purchased as gifts. This was the season of the year when money was secondary to the pleasing of little children. Thus, there are countless Santa figurines available to the collector today. Many beginning collectors become confused by the different terms used to describe this gift-bearing man. Just a brief exploration of his history provides some idea as to the terms applied today on the antiques market.

Santa Claus has his origins in the religious figure of Saint Nicholas, Bishop of Myra, in Asia Minor in the fourth century A.D. St. Nicholas became revered throughout Europe for his good deeds and miracles. He was pictured in white robes, carrying a golden crozier. Later in the sixteenth century, when the Protestant Revolution tarnished his Christian image, St. Nicholas changed his name to Father Christmas in England; Weihnachtsmann, in Germany; and Pere Noel, in France. Father Christmas was a combination of St. Nicholas and pagan predecessors such as Saturn and Thor. Germany's gift bearer was the Christ Child, "Christkind," whose name evolved into Kris Kringle, as the Germans settled in the Pennsylvania German part of our country. To the Pennsylvania Germans, Pelznickel (an old man with a long white beard who armed himself with a switch and carried a bag of toys over his shoulder) was another name for Santa Claus. It was the Dutch who brought St. Nicholas to New York City and it was the Dutch who pronounced this as "Sinter Claes," very close indeed to Santa Claus. However, the greatest transformation of this figure was yet to come.

Washington Irving's *Knickerbocker History of New York*, published in 1809, changed St. Nicholas from a stern bishop into jolly St. Nick who showered gifts and good tidings on the burghers of old Manhattan. The earliest known pictures of Santa's German counterpart are the 1810 engravings by Moritz von Schwind showing a grotesque hooded figure carrying a candle-lighted tree into a snowy Berlin night. In 1815, England's Father Christmas was depicted as a reeling drunken figure with a wreath of mistletoe on his bald head and a steaming wassail bowl in his arms. In 1822, theologian Clement Moore borrowed from Irving's book to write "An Account of a Visit of St. Nicholas," the Christmas poem that begins, "Twas the night before Christmas ..." Thomas Nast's popular illustrations in the mid 1860s created the myths that Santa Claus lived at the North Pole, wore a suit with fur trim, and had a workshop where he made toys.

For almost seventy-five years, there was no change in the characterization of Santa Claus. It was not until the 1930s that his features grew more coarse and his body rotund. It was the Coca-Cola company who humanized Santa, adding blue eyes, bright red lips, and a ruddy complexion. This new Santa Claus was quickly accepted, and is used today across our country on television, in department stores, and for advertising purposes.

Even though we may not be aware of it, many other Santa figures are slightly different due to the fact that each nationality has its own unique representation and history of this gift-bearer. It is important for a collector to be aware of the various histories of Christmas in addition to the German or American versions. Grandfather Frost is the Russian equivalent to our Santa Claus. He is usually old and wears long robes and a flat-crowned hat, typical of the ancient "Rus." Grandfather Frost is usually attired in pale wintry colors, rarely in red. Because Russia has been under an atheistic regime since 1917, Father Christmas is chiefly nonreligious in nature and brings presents on New Year's Day.

Italy is unique in that three different personages have evolved as gift-bearers. On Christmas eve, gifts have been traditionally brought to family members by "Gesu Bambino" (Baby Jesus). The large distribution of gifts is left up to "La Befano," the much revered old witch of olden times, who comes down the chimney on January 5th, the eve of the Feast of the Epiphany.

She is easy to recognize since she always has a straw broom and a sack of goodies. "Babbo Natale," the third personage, is similar to the old German Father Christmas. Italian craftsmen have produced this figure for a period of time from papier-mâché. The cap and robes are formed of paper that has been dipped in a hardening solution so that these figures with flowing robes resemble the Neapolitan creche figures.

Belsnickle, German, height 14", ca. 1910. $1100-1200

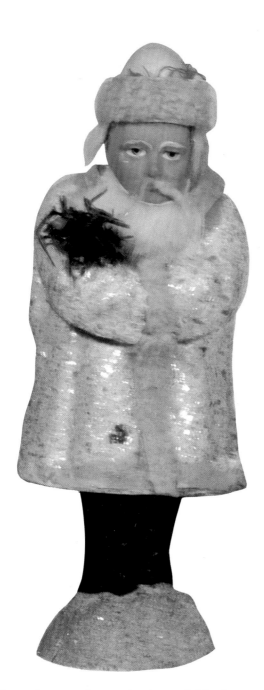

Candy container separating at waist, German, height 9", ca. 1900. $900-1000

Light weight papier-mâché figure, German, height 11", ca. 1920s. $555-650

Candy container with composition face, German, ca. 1930s. $1400-1600

Candy container with flannel clothes and composition boots, German, ca. 1920s. $2000-2300

Candy container, German, ca. late 1920s. $1100-1300

The Scandinavians provide "Jultomten" from Sweden, "Julesvenn" from Norway, and "Julnisse" from Denmark. These are all gift-bearing elves, red-clad figures with pointed caps and long white whiskers. "Jultomten" rides a goat named "Julbock" and "Julnisse" rides "Jul-buken." These goats have pagan roots, being modeled after the goat of Thor that pulled its master's chariot. Most of these Santa type figures are and have been carved from wood for years.

Papier-Mache Santa Figures

Most of the early Santa figures from the Victorian period were constructed from papier-mâché and made in Germany. It was after the Thirty Years War that a French soldier revealed the secret of French-made papier-mâché to a Thuringen toymaker. Collectors commonly refer to these as *belsnickles*. The term originates from "Pelze-Nicol" which literally means "Nicholas dressed in fur." When the north Germans emigrated to the Pennsylvania area in the New World, the pronunciation of this now dreaded figure's name eroded into "Belsnickle." He was feared because he knew all who had sinned from the Christ Child. In Germany, around 1835, the "Weihnachtsmann" first appeared in the form of papier-mâché containers to hold candy, cookies, or small presents.

Papier-mâché, as related to the doll industry in its manufacturing technique, is a mixture of pulp paper, glue, oil, and rosin. Originally, artisans created clay models of Father Christmas, from which negative molds were made. By the mid-1800s, Frederick Muller of Sonneberg added kaolin to the formula, giving strength to the substance and allowing it to be squeezed into molds. This wet mixture was compressed into half-molds. After the two halves dried, the papier-mâché figures were removed, and glued together. The seams were then sanded, and the entire figure sealed with varnish and painted. "Dot" pupil painted eyes, black lid lining, and one-stroke brows in reddish-brown are all characteristics of these early German figurines.

Switches, feather branches, or erikamoos were put into the arms

Butler Brothers, 1905.

George Sommers Company, 1900.

of many of these figures. Rabbit-fur beards, chenille trim, and mica chips were further finishing touches for many of the earlier forms. Red and white are the most common colors for the clothing of these papier-mâché images, with the least common being green, yellow, lavender, pale pink, and blue.

These hollow figures were frequently finished on the bottom with a thin cardboard type base enabling them to stand upright. A few were placed on small square bases which lifted, allowing them to be used as Christmas candy containers. Being a cottage industry, much like that of creating blown glass ornaments, the majority of these figures originated from Sonneberg, the doll center of the world at that time. They came in many sizes. In the 1870s, Butler Brothers imported a show window Father Christmas figure with a feather tree over 21" in height. Made from papier-mâché, the figure became a display piece when the tree was decorated with miniature glass ornaments. When first offered, the price was $1.95, packed for shipment. It is believed that the only customers were retail stores, which purchased them for display purposes. In 1890, Butler Brothers advertised a series ranging from 6" to 17" high, the majority of which seemed to be promoted for home rather than store use. In 1907, L. H. Mace listed 7" to 14 1/2" sizes, with fewer sizes being made in later years. Those which appeared just after World War I were much lighter in weight with thinner walled construction. They were made until the mid-1920s, continuing to be advertised and merchandised by Butler Brothers and Sears Roebuck.

Composition Santa Figures

In addition to these earlier figures, other Santa figures were formed from composition, a form of papier-mâché. Composition has its roots in the 1800s when the Germans manufactured papier-mâché dolls and dolls' heads that were dipped into liquid plaster. The ingredients included dissolved used paper, a glue solution, chalk, heavy spar, and plaster or clay. This mixture was then pressed into a two-part mold and set aside to dry. The composition figures were then dipped in wax or plaster and finally painted.

The most common figural ornament to receive this wax coating was, of course, the waxed angel, popular on the American Christmas tree for almost fifty years. In addition to angels and Santas, there were waxed birds and dwarfs. However, very few Santa figures were waxed, since the majority of these were dipped into a thin coat of plaster. Though some of these were fully molded figures, some had only molded heads, arms, and boots. These parts were attached to a core or a hollow cardboard candy container. Frequently the figure was dressed in velvet or cloth robes. Today, the red has oftentimes faded to a tomato soup-type color. Invariably, these Santa figures were dipped in a thin coat of plaster and finished off with the finest of detail. Santas of this type have very ruddy complexions, stand in stooped postures, and are most often dressed in velvet suits of blue, green, white, and red—these colors being arranged from most rare to the most common.

Those after 1900 can be identified since they most often wore felt clothing rather than the canton flannel popular before 1900. Flannel did not cease to exist after 1900, it just became more rare with the passage of time. After World War I, leather belts were used in lieu of silk, cotton, or other threaded cords. Rabbit fur and lamb's wool were used as trim for the clothes, with rabbit fur used solely for beards. At first the fur was attached directly to the face; later, it was attached to a piece of adhesive tape which was then glued to the plaster coated face. Many of these figures were produced by the old German firm of Herman Wirth, Neustadt.

In 1920, and continuing into the mid-1920s, Japan exported to the United States a number of composition faced, white cotton bearded and clothed Santa figures that are often mistaken by collectors for German types. This 12" Santa was completely covered with cotton, wore an overcoat and hood, had black feet and composition boots, and is found holding a holly handled moss basket. The face is composition with a great deal of molding and painted details. Unfortunately, these figures have not all weathered the ravages of time, for the bond between the papier-mâché and the plaster is not very strong and the plaster easily chips from careless handling and humidity.

Later Japanese manufactured figures (1930s through 1950s), can sometimes be identified by the existence of cotton beards, which became common at that time. These Japanese figures can also be easily identified through their reddish, clay-based faces and cotton molded hands. Those made in the 1920s have clay-based faces, but the coloring is more flesh tone in appearance. In addition, detailed puffy cheeks and frown lines are prominent. Detailed composition faces are characteristic of the 1920s manufactured figures, with later manufactured ones lacking deeply furrowed faces and intricate line detail. Starting in the 1960s, these figures used pressed cardboard faces, on which printed face details were added. Details such as black eyes and simple white lines to show age were the only embellishments. All these figures had composition faces and boots made with a clay base. Japanese figures can be further identified if robes of cotton wadding, flannel, or crepe paper are used. The Japanese also relied heavily on the use of chenille or pipe cleaners, maribou, and foil or paper. Brush trees were usually in the hands of these figures. This is in contrast to the German figures, which always carried trees made of dyed goose feathers.

SANTA CLAUS SHOW PIECE
In big demand for window and holiday displays.

F9864—12 in., composition face, white cotton beard, painted features, black feet and boots, snow covered white cotton overcoat and hood, figure holds holly handled basket containing 3 gifts. 1 in box.
Each, $1.00

Butler Brothers, 1922.

Pressed Cardboard Santa Figures

A later type of papier-mâché figure appeared on the market in the 1920s, manufactured from cardboard which resembled old egg-carton material. The majority of these were manufactured in the United States, but a few were made in Japan and Germany. Pulp Reproduction Company of Milwaukee, Wisconsin, was one of the principal producers of these pressed cardboard Santas. Heavily pressed millboard quite similar to fiberboard or layers of paper saturated with water, were pressed into a mold or shaped over a wooden form. They were heat-dried, dipped into a solution of linseed oil and tar, and baked again. Finally, the forms were varnished, lacquered, and painted. This method produced figures with a shiny finish. Earlier figures do not shine because they were not varnished and lacquered, just simply painted after being baked. These were flat or three-dimensional. The flat ones were meant to be stood upright with cardboard easels stapled to the figure. Used either for store advertising, calendars, or for home decorations, these flat figures were painted with an air brush, giving them a soft tone finish. Frequently, they were embellished with glitter. Deeply embossed, these figures almost appear three-dimensional. If one looks carefully, "Germany" and later "Made in Germany" can be seen embossed on the lower part of the figure. Collectors should be aware that these were manufactured into the 1950s; therefore, look for "Made in West

Pressed cardboard stand-up, German, ca. mid-1930s. $100-125

Pressed cardboard stand-up, German, ca. early 1920s. $150-175

Elaborate pressed cardboard stand-up, German, ca. 1920s. $100-120

Pressed cardboard stand-up, German, ca. early 1920s.
$250-300

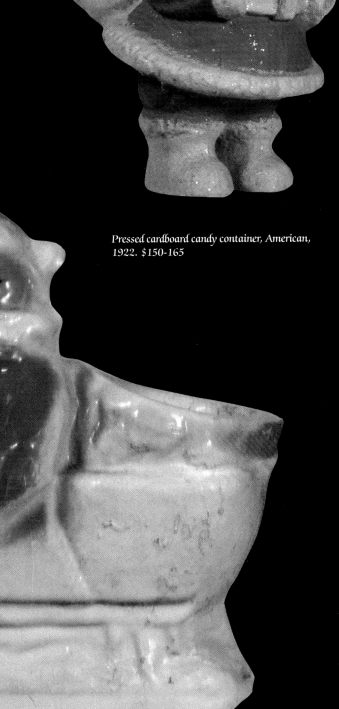

Pressed cardboard candy container, American,
ca. 1940s. $100-120

Pressed cardboard candy container, American,
1922. $150-165

Germany" to indicate such a figure. There is a variety of forms ranging from simple standing figures to scroll messages to Santa riding in an airplane or train engine.

The majority of the American three-dimensional figures served as candy containers with openings in the back for insertion of the candy. Simple standing figures of Santa are the most common, with Santa in a fireplace being the most rare. The most desirable are the Santa riding in the sleigh variations. These seem to come in two distinct color categories. Either the predominant color will be white with red or green trim, or red will predominate with small additions of red and facial tones. A variety of snowmen figures were also manufactured. After World War II, exports from Germany of pressed cardboard figures included large shipments of candy containers with distinctive ball-shaped bodies, ball-shaped heads capped by paper cones, and half-sphere feet. All surfaces with the exception of the face and fur beard were covered with paper plush. When moved, their heads wobbled on head springs and usually the figures separated at the body cavity to reveal a container for candy. Later figures can be identified by a "Made in Germany, U.S. Zone" (1947) marking and later by the marking, "Made in Western Germany." In Neustadt, the firm of M. Grempel, successor to August Schelhorn, brought production to a close in 1965 as a direct result of America's fascination with plastic.

Pressed cardboard candy containers, American, ca. 1940s. Left, $100-110; Right, $135-150.

Pressed cardboard candy containers, West German, ca. 1950s. Left to right: $100-120, $120-140, $150-165.

Pressed cardboard figures, American, ca. 1950s. Left, $75-85; Right, $65-75.

Since these date from the 1920s, collectors should note that the earlier Santas are more slender and colored much more delicately. Beginning in the mid-1930s, these figures were very robust, in imitation of the Santa Claus portrayed in Coca Cola ads. It seems that the most colorful variety of figures were earlier than the predominant white ones. The natural cream colored, slender figures trimmed with red are among those manufactured in the 1920s.

Chalkware and Plaster Santa Figures

An often neglected but quite fascinating figure is the figure which was manufactured from chalkware. The earliest and most unusual of these originate in the Pennsylvania Dutch area of our country. The figures were formed in molds made of plaster or earthenware. To make a chalkware piece, the craftsman first lubricated the inside of the mold with green soap or leather dressing and then tied or clamped shut the mold. The mold was then filled with a thin mixture of plaster of paris poured into the cavity through a hole in the bottom. After the form was removed, the rough mold seams were filed down. The value of such pieces are determined by their condition. Plaster of paris chips and cracks easily and many have been clumsily repaired. Most early Father Christmas figures are found wearing the somber, snow-trimmed coat traditional in the German homeland of the Pennsylvania Dutch. These chalkware figures are most often finished with blue or brown clothing, with red being most desired in this period of time.

Among the most unique plaster-made Christmas items are the Christmas lights in the shapes of a human head, the most common being the Father Christmas head. Manufactured between 1890 and 1910, these were meant to hang on tree limbs. All of these were formed in wooden molds, painted, and finished. Eyes and mouths were lightly plastered so candle light would shine through. In spite of their heaviness, they made a brilliant sight with a candle inside. In this category are Father Christmas full-headed masks to be worn with red robes to impersonate him. These masks have the characteristic lightly plastered eyes and mouths, with thin slits provided for breathing while wearing the mask.

A much later, but equally fascinating chalkware figure was manufactured as a direct result of carnivals and fairs. In the 1930s and the 1940s, for just 10 cents or three tries for a quarter, and a bit of luck, you could carry home a chalkware figure! A number of celebrity figures were manufactured, however Santa Claus was among the most notable and of interest today to Christmas collectors. Most chalkware from the 1930s was distributed by doll and novelty companies. However, for years, many of these were produced by Italian immigrants in mini-assembly lines in garages. Molds were lined up in long rows in these garages with craftsmen pouring a small coating into one of these molds, shaking it, and then continuing onto the next mold, repeating the process until the mold was entirely filled with plaster of paris. Upon occasion, these figures were kept hollow and a slit made in the top of the figure so that it could serve as a bank. Most commonly seen banks include the 1930s standing Santa by a chimney and the 1950s Santa seated in a plush sofa chair.

In keeping with the "inexpensiveness" of these later objects, vermiculite was frequently added to the plaster to act as a filler. The final product was allowed to dry and finished with paint. The details on many of these are quite indistinct and crudely attached, since they were turned out in such great quantity. The most desirable are those which were painted by airbrush.

Chalkware figure, American, ca. early 1940s. $450-550

15

Chalkware figures, American, left: late 1940s, $120-130; right: 1950s, $145-155.

Carnival type chalkware, American, ca. 1930s. Left, $140-150; Right, $160-170.

Celluloid figures, Japan, 1920s and 1930s. Left to right: $95-100, $140-160, $180-210, $220-240, $170-190, $100-110.

Celluloid Santa Figures

Celluloid items date back to the late 1870s. Those most commonly found today date from post World War I. It was John W. Hyatt who developed the formula by mixing pulp from the cotton plant with solvents and camphor. Collectors use "celluloid" as a generic term for all early plastics. Earlier pieces have a creamy color with striations meant to imitate the texture of ivory or bone.

The Germans were among the first manufacturers of celluloid Christmas items. As early as 1895, the Lenel Bensinger Company of Mannheim was stamping its products with the familiar turtle mark. Another German company, Rheinische Gummi-Celluloid Fabrik, also made numerous celluloid Santa figures. These Santa figures are quite rare, and a collector should always check for German marks, which are usually found on the upper back or at the bottom of one foot. Germany gradually phased itself out of celluloid sales due to American competition, and, later, Japanese competition commencing in the 1920s.

Celluloid Santas ranging from two to fourteen inches high were manufactured by the thousands in Japan. These can be identified by an embossed mark in the back. Japanese marks include a quarter moon with star (mid-1920s), a circular tree design inscribed with "Made in Japan" (1930s), "Made in Occupied Japan" (early 1950s), and countless others. Standing figures of Santa are the most common, with toy ladened figures being more rare than Santa holding a lantern. Among the most desirable are Santa with airplanes, cars, trains, sleds, and motorcycles. Of this type, Santa as part of a sleigh and reindeer set is the most common; however, the smaller sleigh with two reindeer is extremely rare. The earliest sleigh sets were produced entirely of celluloid with perhaps metal bells or string added to connect the reindeer and the sleigh. The later, 1940s variety were mounted on a piece of thin wood, fiberboard, or cardboard.

American companies also produced celluloid items for Christmas displays, and the Newark, New Jersey, firm of John W. Hyatt was one of the first. Irwin and Company, located in Chicago and New York, was one of the principal manufacturers of the modern variety found most often today by collectors. The quality of these American items is superior: excellent molding, vibrant colors, and almost perfect detail. Earlier celluloid items from the 1920s are the most carefully detailed and multi-colored, whereas the 1950s items were almost entirely red Santas with only white trim and black eyes. Most of these are single figures, with Santa on skis being the most rare.

The 1950s marked the end of the celluloid era in Christmas decorations. The rarity of such figures is apparent, since celluloid was extremely flammable and easily bent. Thus, few excellent examples have survived and these are beginning to slowly appear on the antiques market, quite reasonably. However, their rarity is insured by their whimsical creativity and fragility.

Collectors become somewhat confused by the age of celluloid items. It would be impossible to cover in detail these items since they were manufactured for quite a long period. However, it can be said that the majority of those found are Japanese in origin and most date from the late 1930s and 1940s. The appearance of the items themselves is a final determining factor of age. The early forms are, of course, more slender in appearance, more intricately detailed, and more carefully painted than those of the 1950s. In addition, early celluloid found today is much thinner and almost brittle in texture.

Butler Brothers, 1925.

2F9541

Santa Claus, painted features, costume and shoes. 1 doz. in box.
2F9541 — 5 in. high.
Gro   Doz T. O.

Butler Brothers, 1932.

1F-9340 — 1 doz. in box.
Doz 78c
2 styles, 7 in. Santa Claus, painted red coat and hood, white beard, toys.

17

American celluloid, ca. 1930s and 1940s. Left to right: $60-75, $160-175, $75-85, $90-100.

Celluloid Max and Moritz, Germany, ca. 1920s. Left, $420-450; Right, $420-450.

Celluloid nodder, Japan, ca. 1930. $325-400

Plush Dressed Rubber Santa Figures

Somewhat ignored by collectors (except for Coca-Cola enthusiasts) are the rubber faced, plush dressed Santa figures that were produced by the thousands, starting in the early 1950s into the 1960s. These were advertised by Sears Roebuck in 1966 as stuffed with cotton to be used as a decoration or as a child's bedmate. These Santas can be characterized by smiling rubber faces, plush beards, and red plush bodies decorated with simulated leather belts.

The earliest of these were manufactured in Japan and included musical varieties that would play a variety of Christmas tunes. Most of these had an entire molded rubber head with good molding and exquisite detail. Those from the 1960s had only faces of rubber, to which a red hood and white beard were sewn. Earlier examples also came with rubber boots and hands, with the Santas of the 1950s having entire bodies of plush. A great number of these were used to merchandise Coca-Cola, with the doll being a promotional device at Christmas. Being of a larger size, these were made with a small bottle of Coca-Cola in his clasped right arm. Many others were used for advertising purposes in stores as part of displays promoting items from watches to pots and pans. An entire category of plush Santas became toys ringing bells and skating across the floors of our homes throughout the country on Christmas morning. There were wind-ups as well as battery operated Santa figures. One had eyes that lit up intermittently while simultaneously moving his hand up and down to ring a bell while rotating on a tin lithographed globe.

While found in some abundance today, these plush Santa figures are destined to become collectors' items due to the plush velvet material which soils and tears somewhat easily and the disposable climate of Americans during the 1950s and 1960s. Especially probable to be rare are the larger ones intended as advertising gimmicks by American merchandisers.

Plush Santas—left: 1950s; right: ca. 1960s. Left, $75-85; Right, $60-70.

Plastic Santa Figures

Almost totally unexplored Santa figures are those manufactured from plastic in the 1950s and 1960s. These will become more attractive as individuals realize the rarity of these items due to the times. After World War II, Americans gained a sense of national pride and purchased American made Christmas decorations. However, the prosperity of this period led to the disposal of many of these plastic figures. Primarily constructed from red, green, or white plastic, these figures served as tree decorations, candy containers, and table top decorations. Numerous styles of Santas and sleighs pulled by reindeer were created with multitudes of Santas on skis being used as containers for hard suckers. Regardless of composition and style, figures of Santa Claus are an exciting category of Christmas collecting. With some diligent searching, many unique figures can be found in a complete range of prices from the economical to the expensive.

Plastic candy containers, American, ca. 1950s. Left, $50-60; Right, $75-90.

Plastic automobile, American, ca. late 1960s. $150-175

Plastic sleighs, American, ca. 1950s and 1960s. Top to bottom: $40-50, $60-70, $35-45, $70-90, $80-90.

Chapter 2
CHRISTMAS AND ADVERTISING

One area of delightful collecting is that of Santa and Christmas themes as employed in advertising. Santa has been used in advertising to sell a multitude of products from Coca-Cola to diesel trucks. In fact, not even such familiar trademarks as Aunt Jemima, the Cream of Wheat chef, and Cracker Jack's sailor boy have enjoyed the same exposure as Santa. N. K. Fairbanks Co. even named a commercial laundry soap for Santa Claus. Trade cards were among the first form of American advertising to employ this characterization, followed by color advertisements with the increased publication of magazines. Santa, used as a part of magazine advertising, did not occur until the 1890s. What few appearances he did make were mostly in children's magazines such as *St. Nicholas* and *Youth Companion*.

Very rare are the first magazine advertisements with Santa selling a product. One advertising campaign for soap did pave the way for subsequent uses of Santa as a "super salesperson." In 1897, a Christmas advertisement of Pears' Soap illustrates a little boy bolting upright in bed, a bar of soap in his hand, surprising Santa with a question: "Good Morning Santy! Have you used Pears' Soap?"

By 1900 Santa was a regular pitchman in household weeklies, selling everything from Cream of Wheat to New Home sewing machines. Another early advertising Santa was the large stand-up cardboard German manufactured Santa, made so colorful and popular with the perfection of German chromolithography. This stand-up figure is usually large, 30-40 inches in height, and shows Santa in a blue coat posed with a multitude of Christmas toys and children. Commercial illustrators, working from 1910 onward, were responsible for dramatically changing the red-suited elf into a jolly, happy-go-lucky salesman. Whatever the product or service, Santa served as an endorsement for its worth. Even the United States government employed this special salesperson. During World War II, Santa sold war bonds in the United States and Chesterfield cigarettes to the servicemen overseas.

The greatest change in Santa's appearance started in the 1930s with his appearance in Coca-Cola ads. Hadden Sundblom, who freelanced with Coca-Cola from the 1930s to the late 1960s, receives the credit for creating the modern version of this now lovable, grandfatherly gift-giver as we know him today. Haddon Hubbard Sundblom was born June, 1899, in Michigan. He quit school at 14; and by the time he was 19, Sundblom was certain that being an artist was his destiny. Enrolling at the American Academy in Chicago, he studied there for four years. This was followed by an additional four years at the Art Institute of Chicago. Though he is most famous for his Santa Claus advertisements for Coca-Cola (each of which was a full size oil painting), he illustrated calendars and many magazine stories.

Sundblom's first Santa advertisement appeared on the back cover of *National Geographic* in December, 1931. This began a series which lasted until 1946. The Sundblom Coca-Cola Santa appeared on posters and other company advertising materials, as well as, Coca-Cola premiums, such as trays. Hundreds of flat stand-up figures of Santa selling Coca-Cola are available to collectors. Since this period, other artists' illustrations have come to resemble Sundblom's interpretations. Santa is now always portrayed as a regular nice guy and the endless scenes of him comfortably at home is almost Norman Rockwell in appearance.

The 1950s found American stores and companies using three-dimensional Santas with plastic faces and distinctive rayon or velvet suits to promote many products. Even though flat cardboard Santas continued to be employed, dolls and other 3-D figures gradually emerged as being more eye-appealing.

SANTA CLAUS.

Put in your window with your Christmas display. Note results.
4 F 2 7 9 3— Solid wood front and back, 13x11½ linen brick effect front, frosted top, cardboard mantel and fireplace with candlesticks and stockings, 8x10 litho Santa face with rolling eyes. Each,
$1.75

Butler Brothers, 1911.

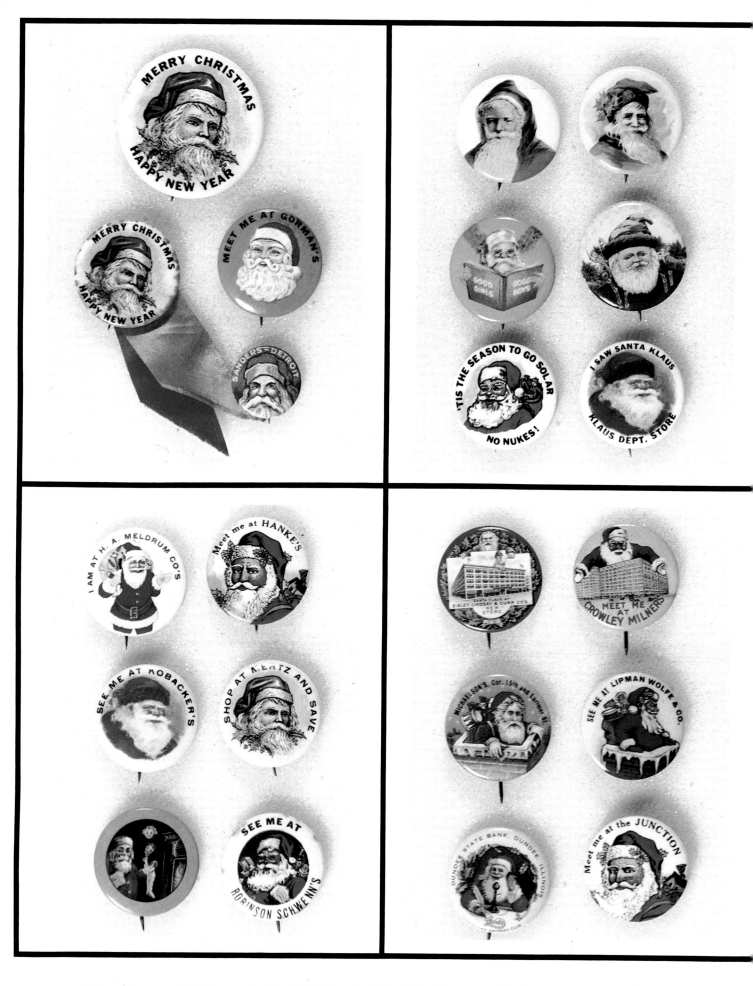

Variety of giveaway celluloid buttons. Top left, $120-135 ea., Top right, $150-175 ea., Bottom left, $165-185 ea., Bottom right, $200-225 ea.

Celluloid and Paper Giveaways

With the advent of celluloid, pin-back buttons became common. The button, made with a clever hoop spring that snapped into the back, was a popular advertising medium for everything from flour to pianos and stoves. Santa Claus bottoms, given away at Christmas by department stores and banks, are a subspecialty among general button collectors and a real delight to Christmas collectors. The majority of pin-back buttons were produced by Whitehead & Hoag who patented the first in 1896; American Artwork of Coshocton, Ohio; the St. Louis Button Company; and Bastian Brothers of Rochester, New York. Occasionally their names may still be found on the small circle of paper which was pressed into the back of the button along with a patent number and date. This gives the collector a clue as to the age of that particular button. Many, such as Santa Christmas Seal buttons, are part of a set and it becomes a challenge to find the complete series.

Some of the rarest celluloid Santa items are the celluloid-back pocket mirrors, meant to be carried in women's purses. Celluloid was used also for measuring-tape cases, bookmarks, shoe horns, stamp cases, pin holders, and matchsafes.

Advertising Giveways

Over the years a multitude of different items designed as advertising giveaways from local banks, insurance agencies, and various stores were used at Christmas. Many of these employed a representation of Santa Claus. Some are easy to find, others are rare, and it is not unusual for a sought-after tray or pocket mirror to garner a price of one thousand dollars or more. Such items have been made of metals, mother-of-pearl, celluloid, paper, china, and plastic. Hand fans made of paper, cardboard, straw, and celluloid were produced and used in abundance. These were given away by the thousands to church groups, funeral parlors, and fraternal organizations and carried home from social and sporting events so often that it is a rare estate that does not contain one or two examples.

Fine German Christmas china, ca. early 1900s. Plate, $175-200; Cup & saucer, $110-140.

Metal Giveaways

Numerous metal objects were also manufactured as advertising giveaways. Advertising trays are the most common, being round, oval, or rectangular. Even though beer and Coca-Cola are the most appealing, Christmas trays were extremely important due to their seasonal usage. The Tuscaron Company and the Standard Advertising Company started manufacturing trays in Coshocton, Ohio, in the 1880s. Subsequent mergers and separations resulted in the Meek & Beech Company, then the H. D. Beech Company, and finally the Meek Company at the turn of the century. In 1909, the Meek Company turned into American Artworks and after 1930, their trays were marked

Silver and china giveaways, ca. early 1900s. Left to right: $120-130, $90-100, Cup, $75-85, Knife, $150-175.

Very early ledger—1885. $210-230

"American Colortype Company." Trays signed by a well-known illustrator are the most treasured with further value being set by age. The first trays were produced by tin lithography, a time consuming process which resulted in a much richer and more brilliant color than those applied by the photolithographic process which became commonplace at the time of World War I. Other metal giveaways included pocket knives, pocket knife cases, folding scissors, button hooks, money clips, and lapel pins. Many of these items were silver-plated.

Multitudes of paper items from bookmarks to comic books were produced at Christmas. Children's booklets, many of them beautifully printed, have also had a history of being used as Christmas giveaways. Some were coloring books; others were books of rhymes, stories, and fairy tales. Countless chocolate mugs and saucers were popular items for little children. China, in the form of plates, was also very popular, with many designed as calendars for a particular year. Complete sets of Christmas related china have been produced over the years as advertising giveaways.

Glass candy tray and container. Left, $100-110; Right, $175-185.

Advertising Calendars

Especially desirable to collectors of Christmas memorabilia are those calendars which illustrate Christmas trees, Santas, or Christmas celebrations. Calendars were chief among advertisements first used in America. The French are credited with their use in the mid-1800s. The "almanac des Poste et Telecommunications" made beautiful calendars each year that were merchandised by postmen. In the 1870s, as a result of the American free enterprise system, free calendars began to be produced. From this time on, beautifully chromolithographed calendars could be found in virtually every American kitchen, reminding each family each day of a product or a store. Insurance companies such as Hartford and Prudential produced calendars with ever-popular subjects, such as children, women, and animals. Some of the most artistically beautiful were given away by the Metropolitan Life Insurance Company. Most of these early calendars are of paper with the most rare being produced from china or celluloid. Air-brushed, beautifully colored, pressed cardboard Santas and Christmas scenes are often found today minus the calendar, since they continued to be used as a decoration when the calendar expired at the end of the year. First manufactured in the 1930s, they continued to be produced through the 1950s in Western Germany.

Numerous ceramic and glass calendar plates were made in the early 1900s when painted flower plates were popular wedding and Christmas presents. The majority of these marked the giver (store or company name) in simple gold letters on the front of the plate. The most common are the Christmas flower ones with Santa scenes being the most desirable for the collector.

Pressed cardboard calendar top, German, 1920s. $80-90

Pressed cardboard calendar top, German, 1930s. $80-90

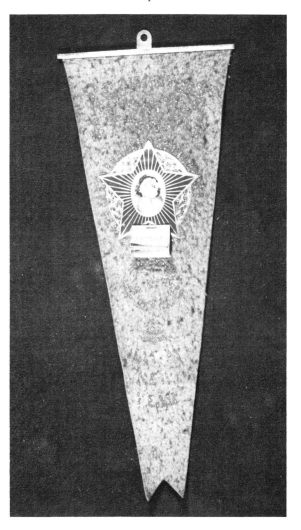

Calendar, Germany, 1911. $100-110

Pressed cardboard advertising, top: German, $90-100; bottom: West German, $75-85.

Advertising calendar top, German, early 1900s. $125-140

Trade Cards

Woolson Spice card, 1880s. $55-65

Woolson Spice card, 1890s. $60-70

Elaborate trade card, ca. late 1800s. $325-375

Deeply embossed trade card, ca. late 1800s. $450-500

Trade card, ca. 1800s. $45-55

Prang card, ca. 1880s. $40-50

Advertising Trade Cards

A large category of advertising giveaways is that of trade cards. Trade cards, the advertising of yesteryear, were a powerful advertising medium, partly because they were also popular entertainment. These cards were collected and pasted into scrapbooks as well as traded between children and women. Insurance companies were among the first to use "canvassing" cards. These were distributed by the company's agents when they collected the weekly premium to placate the payment of precious pennies by families with few to spare. Trade cards were soon handed to a customer in a store, wrapped inside a purchase, left on counters to be picked up, or inside the products themselves.

These cards were used by national and regional manufacturers of all types, and they were given to potential customers. Trade cards appeared at a time when a large number of new products were being "pitched" to the American public and when inexpensive color printing had been perfected. It can be safely said that the majority of Santa Claus and Christmas-scene trade cards were general, all-purpose types, which were printed and sold in wholesale quantities by many different businesses.

The boom of the trade card business seems to have been started with the Centennial Exposition of 1876 in Philadelphia. There is a popular unconfirmed story that a collector who went to the show picked up every trade card he could locate and left the Exposition with over 50,000 different types. Regardless of the authenticity of such a story, trade cards were in abundance at the Exposition and many of these are found today glued into scrapbooks.

A few trade cards were published by individual companies with the illustrations having a direct correlation with their products. Woolson Spice Company of Toledo, Ohio, was a company who manufactured such insert premiums. They were usually five by seven inches and found inside each pound of their Lion coffee. These were made available to the public for several years, beginning around 1881 and continuing into 1897. Alvin M. Woolson, General Manager and principal leader of this company, was responsible for his firm issuing some of the most elegant of all 19th century cards. He employed the best lithographers including Knapp and Company, Bufford, and Donaldson Brothers, with his earliest printer being George Harris and Sons of Philadelphia. Executed in soft pastels, these cards were found in packages between the middle of October and the end of the year. Each year the scenes changed from colorful portrayals of Santa Claus, to children asleep on the night before Christmas and many other types of images which captivated the imagination of that Victorian period. These cards are extremely rare today since printing runs were relatively small and undoubtedly residual stocks were destroyed at the end of each calendar year.

One of Mr. Woolson's principal competitors, the Arbuckle Bros. Coffee Company, also produced lavish Christmas advertising cards to sell their product, forcing the price of coffee down quite quickly to 15 cents a pound!

Today collectors especially prize the cards of preeminent print makers such as Currier and Ives as well as L. Prang and Company. Physical size, subject material, and condition affect the value. The larger cards, up to twelve inches, are far more valuable than those two to four inches in size. Subject material is a further determination of worth for a card which merely shows a flower or winter scene is not nearly as valuable as a card illustrating an old-fashioned decorated tree with little children. The most desirable are those which incorporate Santa Claus, with full figures once again more desirable than half figures.

A trade card that is bent, stained or trimmed has less value than one in perfect condition. Many old cards were pasted in scrapbooks,

and removing them without damage is difficult. Soaking the pages and then lifting the wet cards out is a technique used by some; however, this method does do harm regardless of the care taken. Some collectors have been successful putting the scrapbooks in a freezer. After a few days, the scrapbook is removed and the cards lifted from the paper. This method seems to work best for flour and water type paste.

By the early 1900s, cards became smaller and not as well printed. Photography had entered the designs, and slogans replaced the almanac-like information on the backs of these early cards. Scraplike trade cards were given away with periodicals, or by stores to advertise products. Quite quickly, almost as fast as they had appeared on the American advertising scene, trade cards disappeared from use. Even though trade cards in general are in abundance, true Christmas representative trade cards are indeed quite rare today.

Thus, it is this "pleasantly plump" fellow who began to be used as the number one salesman, endorsing every conceivable product from early fall until December 25th. An exciting category exists for any Christmas enthusiast who desires to amass a collection of Christmas advertising.

New York business trade card, late 1800s. $100-125

Front: Ice cream advertising, late 1800s. $500-550

Back: milk advertising.

Soap box, late 1800s. $500-600

Lion coffee poster, late 1800s. $750-850

Large elaborate Sapolin poster. $1500-1750

Large cardboard stand-up, 1920s. $1250-1400

Cardboard stand-up, 1920s. $600-650

Checkers advertising, 1920s. $800-850

Candy tin, early 1940s. $130-145

Candy tin, early 1950s. $90-100

Candy tin, 1930s. $140-160

Electric light set, 1920s. $90-100

1930s poster. $225-240

1920s light set. $60-65

Candy and Biscuits

Early lithographed tins. Left to right: $325-350, $400-450, $420-440.

Early handled tins. Left to right: $100-125, $220-240, $165-185.

Rare early advertising pails. $400-450 ea.

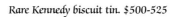
Rare Kennedy biscuit tin. $500-525

Wooden cigar box, 1920s. $100-125

Elaborate lithographed candy box. $90-100

Wooden box, 1920s. $130-150

Cigar box, early 1920s. $120-140

Cigar box, 1920s. $150-180

Wooden box, possibly for cigars. $100-110

Cigar box, 1930s. $140-160

Toffee tin, late 1920s. $225-240

SANTA SELLS SODA

Pepsi-Cola stand-up, late 1940s. $225-250

Stand-up, 1940s. $230-250

Stand-up, 1950s. $220-240

Stand-up, 1950s. $250-265

Stand-up, 1940s. $290-310

Stand-up, 1940s. $300-325

7up stand-up, 1950s. $120-140

Coke and Fresca stand-up, 1960s. $185-200

Coke and Sprite poster, 1960s. $180-200

Chapter 3

CANDY CONTAINERS AND CORNUCOPIAS

Many collectors looking for an area of Christmas specialization have discovered candy containers and many others will turn to this area in the next few years due to the infinite variety of items available. This category can be broken down into figural cardboard containers, commonly called Dresden; figural papier-mâché containers; cardboard candy boxes; net Christmas stockings, cornucopias and other scrap-fronted, tinsel-trimmed containers; netted bags trimmed with celluloid; and the simple rectangular boxes made up through present times.

Dresden Type Candy Containers

Undoubtedly countless candy containers of the Dresden variety were produced between 1880 and up to World War I. At the height of their popularity, hundreds of different candy containers were produced as party favors and for use as Christmas tree decorations and presents. Even though their popularity declined, they continued to be manufactured in smaller quantities and with less detail and exactness, on into just before World War II. These are part of the "Luxious-Papier" industry from 1850 to the present. The manufacturing process consisted of separately prepared cardboard sides which were deeply embossed and then glued together to create a hollow, which could be filled with candy or occasional small presents or favors. Recent historical information seems to indicate that the creation of these Dresden ornaments and containers was a small factory project with the finishing being done by cottage workers. This seems quite feasible when considering the manufacturing process.

In the hollow embossing process used for this, each raised area in the upper stamp (matrix) responded to an identical depression in the bottom stamp (patrix) of the embossing press. These presses were steam powered and similar to those used for embossing and printing of chromolithographs. A slightly damp, relatively elastic sheet of cardboard, or several sheets of thin paper, with glue spread between them, were squeezed by the raised part of the press into the depressed part under great pressure. Cottage workers would then receive these "embossed halves" for finishing.

Their task was to assemble the individual parts, carefully gluing the stamped edges of front and back together, smooth out these "seams," and paint, silver, and gild the objects, unless metal covered material had been used. Prior to 1940 real silver and bronze (so called Dutchgold) leaf was affixed to the stock before embossing. After World War II, only aluminum foil has been used with lacquer to create the gold color. A book about "paper-Specialties" published in 1896 spoke of three-dimensional objects of paper as follows: "The process aims at constructing three-dimensional objects of all kinds, especially objects of

Dresden type heart with silk pouch. $325-350

Dresden violin with opening in back. $350-400

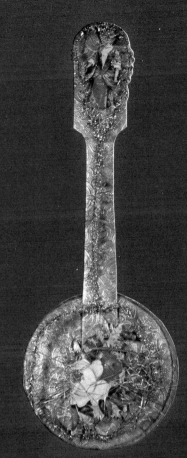

Dresden banjo with opening in back. $350-370

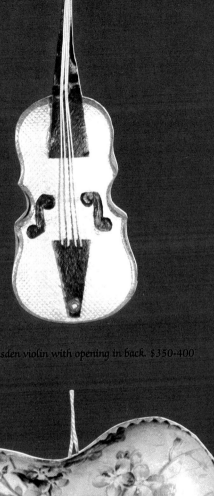

Dresden heart container. $200-220

Dresden canteen container. $285-300

Dresden type candy box. $250-300

Dresden type oval container. $200-225

paper, in such a way that such objects appear as if they had been manufactured of sheet metal." (1)

Musical instruments were among the most popular with Shackmans and Butler Brothers, both advertising guitars, mandolins, violins, and banjos in the 1890s. The tops lifted off to reveal a tiny hollow for candy. These hollows were lined with designed paper or foil.

Some of the simplest of containers were satchels with foreign labels, floral design hat boxes, hearts, curved top trunks, book shaped boxes, imitation leather suitcases, and travel bags complete with paper brass locks and handles. Some of the more rare include baby grand pianos, leather footballs and basketballs, carriages, and ships. An entire host of imitation edibles was produced including peanuts, walnuts, apples, pears, and even a potato.

Almost all of these containers were lined. Most often a simple cream color paper with fleur de Lis was used with lace trim around the edges to provide a most pleasing appearance when opened. The most expensive and prized containers were lined with a candy pouch made from fabric such as silk with draw strings to close the containers. This was often used with animal and human heads. There seems to be no end to the variety of Dresden type candy containers found by collectors today.

Dresden type container. $210-230

Papier-Mache Candy Containers

The second major category includes papier-mâché containers in an infinite variety of forms. The most common figural is that of Father Christmas or Santa Claus. Other shapes include eggs, snowballs, snowmen, bells, fruits, vegetables, animals globes, and boots. Especially popular at the turn of the century and just before were candy boxes made of papier-mâché and coated with wax. More details regarding the specific production of these is contained in Chapter 1.

The most rare include the larger variety of Father Christmas and gift-bearer figures that are Belsnickle in type. One such container, an eleven inch Knect Ruppet, was made in Germany and England in the early 1900s. Most of these figures opened at the base so candy could be inserted. Some were placed on bases which opened to reveal a cavity for candy and even others separated at the waist to reveal a box which could be filled with sweets. The figures were either made entirely of papier-mâché or they were clothed in fabric which covered the candy container itself. These types of Father Christmas containers are the most desirable and command the highest of prices.

More common types of containers were made and are easier for collectors to find today. Many of these types were three to six inches in height and were sold by mail order houses as well as department and specialty stores at Christmas time. Most were hollow with the heads being removed so the cavity could be filled with candy. In 1903, Butler Brothers included an assortment of such containers including rabbits, dogs, pigs, and cats with glass eyes. Another popular candy container of papier-mâché was the reindeer either sold separately or more elaborately as a complete set of Santa, sleigh, and reindeer. All of these deer had removable heads into which the candy could then be inserted. Fruit containers sold at the turn of the century consisted of apples, pears, bananas, oranges, and watermelons in various sizes.

Papier-mâché belsnicklesnicke container, German. $425-460

Papier-mâché lanterns, German (later used as containers). Left to right: $1600-1800, $1500-1700, $1300-1500.

Papier-mâché, Santa with wooden sleigh, German, 1930s. $300-325

Waxed papier-mâché pear container, German, ca. 1905. $475-500

3" papier-mâché candy container, German, early 1900s. $600-650

Many early pressed cotton, figured candy containers opened by means of a circular cardboard disk in the bottom of the container. Another very collectible papier-mâché type container are those made in Germany and Japan which had an oval or circular box on top of which was perched a cotton child, animal, or Santa figure. These cardboard boxes were covered with fabric, mica chips, or merely white paint, and on the top was placed a cotton figure. The earliest and most rare of these was finished with a wax face, with later ones having a bisque, clay, or paper face. Some of the figures are placed on small wooden skis or sleds and found in a variety of different actions. It is possible to find composition Santas on logs, cotton Snow Babies on stumps, and even cotton deer posed with goose feather branches. These were meant more as table favors than as tree decorations and are difficult to find today in pristine condition due to the cotton employed.

Candy box, Japan, 1920s. $175-200

Papier-mâché containers, Germany. Left to right: $500-525, $400-425, $210-230, $210-240, $265-290.

Sleigh container pulled by Dresden deer, Japan. $230-250

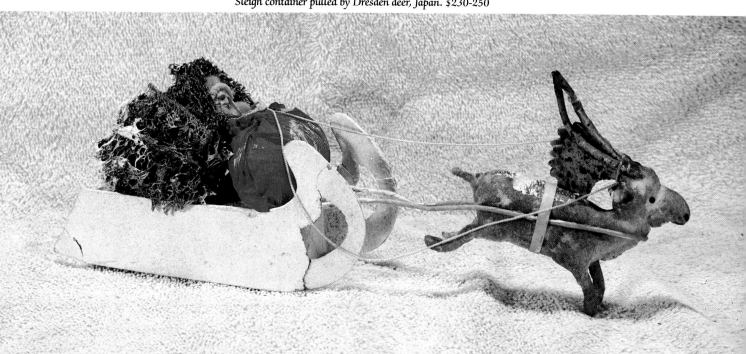

Early papier-mâché containers. Left to right: $700-750, $200-230, $700-750.

*Papier-mâché and cotton (wax head) containers.
Left, $300-325; Right, $400-425.*

After World War I, many other different containers were made including snowballs coated with tiny glass beads. Most were finished with a cotton string for attachment to the tree with the finest of these snowballs being placed on wooden sleds with a papier-mâché Santa riding in the front. Snowballs were also manufactured after the War. Most of these can be easily identified by the more modern chromolithography, the silver glitter trim on the outside, and the inside lining printed with "Made in Western Germany." Metal snowballs with thin metal loops lithographed with Christmas scenes were filled with hard candy and were available as tree decorations in the early 1960s. Bells of papier-mâché were made in the 1920s, but more commonly in the 1930s in Germany. These were filled from the bottom with a removable cone-like insert. Made of papier-mâché, they were heavily covered with glitter and mica chip trim.

Candy box, Japan, 1920s. $230-250

Candy containers, German, 1920s. Left, $435-440; Right, $250-270.

Papier-mâché and cotton containers, ca. 1920. $1400-1600

Papier-mâché containers, mid-1930s. Left to right: $100-125, $90-100, $175-200.

Papier-mâché containers, late 1930s. Left to right: $90-110, $240-260, $175-190.

The most common papier-mâché candy container is undoubtedly the red boot which was manufactured in great abundance. However, the German boot is more desirable than the boots manufactured in Japan and America. The most commonly found boot is the one that has been manufactured by the Milwaukee Pulp Products since the 1930s. Initially the company was named Wisconsin Pulp which pioneered many dozens of holiday items. Later named Pulp Reproductions Company, it was again re-named Carrylite, Inc. which operated between 1965 and 1975. Today this company (Milwaukee Pulp Products, Inc.) still produces boots in three, six, and thirteen inch sizes. Some are sent out white and some are painted red with the cuff white. Small ducks, owls, and mushrooms are also currently produced with larger ducks, mission bells, half-forms, reindeer, and wreaths still being offered for sale.

Papier-mâché boots, American, 1940s. $40-60 ea.

Japanese Candy Boxes

The Japanese manufactured candy boxes which incorporated cotton clay-faced Santa figures. Primarily manufactured in the 1920s and the 1930s, these consisted of paper houses, churches, and towers topped by a cotton Santa with a clay face, carrying a miniature brush tree. The candy was added by means of either the tower or roof lifting off the container itself. Some houses were built over a base which separated at the bottom to provide a receptacle for candy. Advertised by Butler Brothers in 1920, this is one type of container that seems to have been exclusively produced by the Japanese, much earlier than first thought by Christmas historians.

Japanese candy boxes, 1920s. $140-160 ea.

Japanese candy house containers, 1940s. $50-60 ea.

Japanese candy house containers, 1920s and 1930s. $140-165 ea.

Even though these are not candy containers, they are Japanese in origin. Constructed of composition, cloth, papier-mâché and chenille, these figures become more scarce with each passing year. More information regarding these figures is found in Chapter 1.

Japanese figures, 1950s. $40-50 ea.

Occupied Japan Santa. $325-350

Japanese figures, 1930s. $90-100 ea.

Cornucopia with crepe paper top, 1920s. $200-225

Cornucopia, early 1900s. $230-250

Paper Cornucopias and Baskets

Paper cornucopias and other scrap-fronted, tinsel-trimmed containers adorned countless trees over the years, primarily before World War II. This category of containers was popular since they were inexpensive and more easily adaptable for use as tree decorations. Also these containers were more common since they were often given as Sunday school favors or presents at Christmas Eve church services. Considering how fancy and elaborate they usually were, it is amazing that so many have survived the years.

There are basically two cornucopia shapes: the cylindrical and triangular. The cylindrical is the easier of the two for collectors to locate since many of them were manufactured at home from instructions found in various ladies magazines. They most often are decorated with chromolithographs and tinsel sprays with tinsel handles for at-

taching the cornucopia to the tree. The variations found by collectors seems to be infinite with a variety of chromos, tinsel, and foil trim found. The simple, plain, heavy foil type found with a scalloped edge and eyelet for hanging purposes is a product of the 1960s and should not be confused with earlier cylindrical cones. The basket was the most long-lived, being sold well into the late 1920s. These baskets were also trimmed with tinsel sprays, Dresden foil stars and braiding, and were attached to the trees with tinsel wire handles.

The triangular were most often commercially manufactured, thus there were fewer of these in use. Being commercially produced, most all of them had ribbon handles, and being commercially printed, they very seldom had tinsel or chromolithographed trims. These were used for a variety of purposes including Valentine's Day and New Years presents, and it is not uncommon to find them decorated with flowers and hearts as well as with Christmas motifs.

Cornucopia, 1920s. $190-210

Cornucopia, late 1800s. $160-180

Cornucopia, late 1800s. $170-190

Basket, early 1900s. $175-200

Pouch-type candy container, cloth, 1920s. $100-120

Basket, early 1900s (containers in back). $300-325

Basket, 1920s. $190-210

Japanese Net Candy Containers

One of the emerging collectible categories of candy containers is the net bag type container made in Japan. Starting in the 1920s, bags of netting material were made to which celluloid or clay faces, hands, and feet were attached. The earliest of these, from the 1920s, were baskets made of heavy waxed threads topped by a netted bag with a drawstring. Decorating the top of the basket was a celluloid Santa face with a cloth head and cloth arms finished with molded clay hands. The 1930s saw a host of Santa bodied, net bags trimmed with celluloid faces, netted hands and feet finished with clay, and a drawstring in the bag. The only fabric involved was the cloth hat of Santa with glass beads providing trim in the front. Those produced just before World War II incorporated long cloth legs and arms finished with clay. They were further embellished with red fabric sewn in the front. These ranged in size from three to eight inches.

Other Japanese variations of the candy container were either a high boot or a low shoe covered with flannel or silver foil and trimmed with foil leaves and composition berries. Occasionally pipe cleaner trim was also employed. This hollow shoe was topped by a cotton mesh bag with drawstrings. A celluloid face with clay arms at the top of the net bag finished the container. The least common container of this category is the five inch Santa with a paper body encircled with paper chenille ropes, foil-covered suit, and a celluloid face with a cotton beard on top of a net bag. A multitude of other such containers are constantly surfacing and one of the most rare is a cardboard automobile with a net bag top, trimmed with a celluloid head. Containers such as this were produced in Japan and then exported to this country to such companies as the United Candy Company of Boston and St. Louis who then filled these with candy and sold them at Christmas.

Japanese net basket, 1920s. $230-250

Japanese wood sleigh with netting, 1930s. $260-280

Japanese chenille basket, 1930s. $270-290

55

Japanese duck basket, 1920s. $400-425

Japanese net basket, 1930s. $200-215

Japanese automobile container, 1930s. $275-300

Rectangular Candy Boxes

The last category of candy containers are the American printed and produced rectangular boxes most often given on Christmas Eve to children at church services. In the 1920s, one hundred of them could be had for the price of $2.00. At the same time, Butler Brothers sold paper candy baskets printed in Santa designs with paper handles which folded out. Also sold that same year there were Santa Claus chimney candy boxes over thirteen inches high, which incorporated a chromolithograph of Santa with toys coming out of the chimney. These sold for 98 cents a dozen. Dennison Brothers of the U.S. were major distributors of this type of paper candy container. Found more commonly today, they soon also will be joining the ranks of the rare as more and more collectors begin to search out the American products manufactured at Christmas.

American candy box, 1930s. $75-85

American candy box, 1920s. $240-260

Paper candy baskets, American, 1940s. $50-70 ea.

Chapter 4

CHRISTMAS AND THE POWER OF PRINT

A merry Christmas.

Christmas Cards

Many collectors wonder about the beginning of Christmas greeting cards. Some Christmas historians have traced cards back to 18th century schoolboys, who composed intricate letters to their parents to show their progress in penmanship. These early letters were written on hand-decorated paper. It is reputed that parents liked the look of these letters so much that they began to include decorated letters with their Christmas gifts.

Regardless of origin, December, 1843 marks the date of the first commercial Christmas card. The designer was John Horsley who created it at the request of his friend, Sir Henry Cole. There were 1,000 copies lithographed and put on sale in London. Two panels illustrating the feeding of the hungry and clothing the naked so aroused public anger that the cards were withdrawn and the entire venture was termed a flop. Today only twelve of these original cards have been discovered by the collectors. However, in spite of its failure, in succeeding years, the practice of sending Christmas cards grew and even spread to the American continent.

It remained for Louis Prang, a German lithographer who migrated, in 1850, to Roxbury, Massachsetts, to actually popularize greeting cards in the United States. Introducing Christmas cards to America in 1875, he became almost immediately successful due to his color printing process which employed up to 20 plates.

Elaborate fold-out card, German, early 1900s. $260-280

Fold-out, German, ca. 1910. $90-110

Fold-out, German, ca. 1920. $95-110

Prang's early cards followed the then British vogue of humor, flowers, animals, elegant ladies, children, and scenes often unrelated to Christmas. Beetles, spiders, and various birds were often posed among flowers and ribbons with "Merry Christmas" in small letters being the only clue to its original intention. In fact, many collectors often mistake these for valentines since they were so adorned with ribbons, lace, and flowers. In 1880, Prang started offering prizes ranging from $200 to $2,000, to artists for original drawings.

Card designs and their use of Christmas symbols have been diversified over the years. Mistletoe and holly were used on the earliest cards with St. Nicholas making his first appearance in the 1850s. Silk fringe borders became the fad in the 1880s. It took until the late 1890s to find Christmas trees as common illustrations on cards, and the first religious themed cards appeared about the same time. Poinsettias were

virtually unknown until the early 1900s. English card maker Raphael Tuck began to publish Christmas cards in 1871 while American manufacturer George Whitney started card publication in 1877.

During the 1900s, German-made cards began to appear, dominating the market until World War I. Some of the most unique included three-dimensional fold-outs incorporating die-cuts and honeycomb tissue paper. Mechanical cards opened to reveal scrap angels ringing Christmas bells, nativity scenes, tiers of angel heads, gift-adorned trees, and sleeping Victorian children. Butler Brothers advertised cards made into wall pockets which were treasured and kept in albums. However, most popular were the postcard size, which cost a penny and could be mailed with a penny stamp. It was the popularity of this inexpensive postcard that caused Prang to quit designing his elaborate cards in 1897.

Money enclosure card, German, early 1900s. $130-140

These chromolithographed, lavish cards were popular for nearly two decades. It was not until about 1910 that Christmas greetings of the type we know today, appeared on the market. Another important manufacturer of Christmas cards was the George C. Whitney Company of Worcester, Massachusetts. Known more for their valentines, this firm was in business from shortly after the Civil War until 1942. Yet another early important American manufacturer was the Gibson Art Company of Cincinnati, Ohio. For many years, they imported and sold German cards but recognized that these German cards did not reflect American tastes as well as the cards they could design. The firm was headed by three brothers: E. P., C. R., and H. W. Gibson.

In the early 1900s, Christmas cards were seldom signed or mailed; they were delivered in person and left with a calling card. These early Christmas cards were typically very ornate and usually in the form of a bouquet or basket of flowers; ribbons or tabs could pulled up or down from the card to open the flowers and reveal messages of health, happiness, and goodwill. Some cards had ribbons or cords so they could be hung while others were meant to be preserved in ornate frames. Kate Greenaway contributed to greeting card designs as well as doing illustrations for children's books. A designer for Marcus Ward & Company, her "children" are considered to be masterpieces of greeting card art.

The modern greeting card industry began in the early 1900s with the birth of such companies as Hallmark Cards (first known as Hall Brothers Inc.), Rustcraft, Buzza, and American Greetings. Even during the Depression, printed greetings were popular. During that time money was so scarce, that Americans sent cards rather than gave presents at Christmas. Most cards were of heavy cardboard stock with colorful illustrations and a simple verse. Surviving the Depression, the greeting card industry was then challenged by World War II with its curtailed paper supplies. Glitter suddenly became more scarce than gold. Along with the patriotism of the period, Christmas cards, too, became very patriotic. The American flag was often carried by Santa.

The 1940s and 1950s gave us the linen paper card that is destined to become a collectible in its own right. The 1960s and 1970s continued to give us a multitude of variety, with cards often missing Santa as a depiction. It is these Santa cards that will be the collectibles of tomorrow.

In addition to commercial cards, there have been multitudes of home-crafted cards sent over the years. Millions of children created cards from paper, pens, and crayolas that are destined to be discovered. Only the ingenuity of the creator could limit its individuality. Cards have been extremely unique in their history. The smallest Christmas card ever made was a grain of rice inscribed with a 25-word message, given to the British royal family in 1929. Measuring 21 by 33 inches, one of the largest cards ever believed to have been sent was in 1928, to Calvin Coolidge. A more unusual example was a dried codfish skin sent by fishmongers in Gloucester, Massachusetts, to their customers. Novelty cards included birds that actually squeaked or double-headed babies who cried when the miserable side of the face was showing. Many other novelties such as "Talking cards," which today fascinate recipients, are not new since they first appeared in the United States before World War I. They were really miniature records. Just before World War I, the greeting card business was booming with over $81 million dollars worth of cards purchased. Such novelty cards are now among the most rare of Christmas greeting cards. The Christmas card custom has weathered war, economic turmoil, and social changed. It is an outgrowth of our human need to share special thoughts with our friends and relatives far and near during our most cherished holiday season.

3-dimensional German card, early 1900s. $150-175

Another related paper item in this category of cards is the greeting card booklet, very popular among collectors of both Christmas and paper items. Popular in the late 1890s, these normally contained excellent, lavish examples of art work and poetry written by such notables as Longfellow, Tennyson, and Whittier. Meant to be kept as souvenirs, these booklets were a "marriage" of the greeting card and book. Publishers of these cards included Cupples and Leon, Co., Holiday Publishing, Charles E. Graham and Co. of New York City, as well as, Berger Publishing of Buffalo, New York. The range in size from four to twelve pages and are collected more for their signed artist representations than for printed verses.

Large, elaborate chromolithograph sent as a card. $250-270

3-dimensional card, German, late 1800s. $110-120

Postcards

Postcards in Austria were officially sanctioned in 1869. The first commercial picture postcards believed to have appeared were in France in 1870. In America, the government published its first postal card in 1873 which sold for one penny while commercially produced cards needed a two-cent stamp. It was the 1893 World's Columbian Exposition in Chicago that led to the modern postcard when Charles Goldsmith persuaded the United States Post Office to license him to print illustrated souvenir cards of the fair on government postals. Early unmailed postcards can be identified somewhat simply. Until government regulations were altered in 1907, one side of a card was reserved for the address, requiring illustration and message to be crowded onto the other side. While most of the more desirable cards were printed in Europe, high-quality cards were also made in the United States by Detroit Publishing company and Edward H. Mitchell of San Francisco.

FRÖHLICHE WEIHNACHTEN.

Raphael Tuck & Sons, early 1900s. $40-45

Raphael Tuck & Sons, 1908. $60-75

A merry Christmas!

German, 1907. $35-45

German, early 1900s. $30-40

A Happy Christmas

A MERRY CHRISTMAS

German, late 1800s. $50-65

German, late 1800s. $60-70

Fröhliche Weihnachten

German, 1911. $60-75

A MERRY CHRISTMAS

Christmas has been incorporated on postcards from the very beginning; therefore, a whole avenue of Christmas collecting is available to anyone who wishes to specialize in postcards. By 1907, German, British, and domestic postcards alike were being devoured by a most eager American public. Montgomery Ward and Sears Roebuck sold Christmas postcards by the hundreds of thousands for approximately ten years. Since the subject material is so vast for this category, it is strongly recommended that one specialize in a particular theme of Christmas or collect cards illustrated by a particular artist. The most desirable of the artist-signed cards include Frances Brundage and Ellen Clapsaddle. Collectors interested in Christmas history might search for the extremely rare, real black and white photos illustrating past celebrations of this holiday. This category would prove a challenge, for few families could afford the luxury of a professional photographer recording their Christmas. These cards are so fascinating as they illustrate period decorations as well as toys and clothing fashions.

Other suggestions for more inexpensive and easier to find cards might be children at Christmas, winter scenes, fantasy animals, and flowers, for example. Strongly embedded in postcard collecting by enthusiasts, is the notion of collecting Santa postcards. Even though the collecting of such cards is substantial and has been undertaken for years, collectors today can still find many rare and lavish illustrations of this gift-bearer available for purchase.

The most rare of these Santa related cards includes the hold-to-light, transparency, silk, mechanical, and full European figured cards. The hold-to-lights are especially valuable to collectors since they are composed of multiple layers of cardboard, with the top layer containing the picture, cut out at strategic points that corresponded to a Santa figure or scene. Backing these is translucent paper which permits a light source to illuminate the scene. The process was applied to cards

Silk card, German, 1910. $80-90

Silk card, German, 1911. $70-80

Air brush, American, 1907. $35-45

early for HTL's have been found postmarked as early as 1899. The only artist who signed this type of card was Mailick who drew for the firm of D.R.G.M. (Gesetzli). It is felt that as many as two hundred different HTL cards were produced. Transparency postcards are similar to HTL cards in that they contain a blank space in a design that otherwise fills the front of the card. A scene of children decorating a tree will reveal the figure of Father Christmas observing the scene if the card is held up to bright light. These are extremely scarce and are priced accordingly.

Some cards had pieces of silk fabric glued to them while countless others had fringes of silk around the entire card. Most often Santa's clothes and upon occasion, the clothes of children and the hide of animals, were covered with different color silk. The most unusual colors for Santa's robe include brown, white, purple, green, and blue with red being the most common. Mechanical postcards with moving parts are likewise very desirable. Cards were produced which changed the facial expression of Santa according to a tab on top of the card. Other cards manufactured include open and shut eyes, moving arms, and even a moving pack of toys on Santa's back.

In the realm of collecting postcards, the most desirable are artist signed Santa cards, followed by the earlier representations of St. Nicholas in his bishop's clothing, early Father Christmas full figured cards, and those cards which employ Santa Claus with transportation themes.

After World War I, greeting postcards declined quickly in popularity and the later "linen" cards rarely had Christmas themes. Not quite as valuable, but also becoming quite collectible are these cards from the late 1920s through the mid-1930s. Countless books have been devoted to the postcard and it is recommended that collectors interested in pursuing the acquisition of these cards avail themselves of further reading for the world of postcards allows for vast collecting possibilities.

Christmas Related Books

Assembling a collection of children's Christmas books is relatively simple due to the large amount of books published on the subject. Many of those first printed were of Christmas plays (published by Baker Publishing), but later, most were editions of "The Night Before Christmas" sometimes titled, "A Visit from Saint Nicholas." The poem itself appeared in 1823, but it was not until 1845 that it was first published. The first illustrated edition, subtitled *A Present for Good Little Boys and Girls* was printed by Henry W. Onderdonk in 1848 with wood engravings by Theodore C. Boyd. This was later reproduced in 1934 by Dodd, Mead and Company and again by Dover Publications in 1971.

In 1862 F.O.C. Darley illustrated a booklet, and shortly afterward Nast's first black and white drawings of Santa Claus were included in the book *Christmas Poems*.

After the Civil War, Christmas booklets and soft bound books for children began appearing. Among them was *The Night Before Christmas*, the title by which Moore's original story is now known. By the 1880s and 1890s, the publishing effort became a veritable tide as one firm after another aggressively marketed editions of the beloved classic. All of these were lavishly illustrated with large drawings depicting the progression of the tale and each usually had colorful lithographic covers. Some collectors especially seek out books published by Raphael Tuck, Saalfield, M. A. Donahue, McLoughlin Brothers, Nister, and George Whitney because these publishers created some of the most artistic, creative, and well-colored books during this period. McLoughlin Brothers was a major American producer of children's books, producing die-cut and linen books of remarkable quality. One such example was published in 1896, which pictures on the cover a train, ball, Noah's ark, bicycle, and sled complete with a setting of a lavishly decorated Christmas tree. Other American publishers included the Homewood Publishing Company and W. E. Conkey of Chicago as well as Charles E. Graham and M. A. Donahue of New York.

Many Christmas books were written for children but some may be found that are designed for adult reading. *Christmas in Art and Song*, a charming hard-covered book put out by the Arundel Printing and Publishing Company in 1880. There are illustrations by John Gilbert, Raphael, Rubens, Thomas Nast, and unsigned prints as well. In 1923, the Hatch Music Company of Boston was selling a ten page booklet which set Moore's poem to music. It was illustrated by Grace Drayton, creator of the Campbell Kids. The music itself was composed by Hanna van Vollenhoven and copyrighted by the Boston Music Company. The booklets were sold for 75 cents each, a comparatively high price for that time. Hallmark offered an unusual illustrated version of St. Nicholas in *The Night Before Christmas* in 1935. The entire publication was populated with characters from the comic strip owned by United Features Syndicate. Popeye, Blondie, Jiggs and Maggie, and the cast from Flash Gordon joined Santa to tell the story.

Collectors who find the elaborate, early, lithographed books to be too scarce, can collect a multitude of Christmas books. Bound volumes of *St. Nicholas* magazines are filled with Christmas lore, especially the December and January issues. The early *Christmas Ideals*, published in Wisconsin in the early 1940s, are also collector's items today. These *Christmas Ideals* issues contain various artistic representations of Christmas and Santa Claus in addition to recipes, historical references, and photographic recordings of Christmas celebrations. Large numbers of carol, hymn, recipe, and craft books were also published over the years and make interesting acquisitions outlining past Christmas festivities.

Tin book, German, early 1900s. $350-400

Pop Up Books and Mechanical Paper Toys

Pop-up books had their beginnings as early as 1540 when an astronomy text was created with elaborately engineered cardboard machinery which revolved stars and planets through the clockwork heavens. Dean and Son of Treadneedle Street in London, who pioneered in the creation and distribution of lithographs for children's books, began to fashion mechanical books in 1856. Ernest Nister of London, the English market representative of the Nister Company of Nuremberg, Germany, also quickly joined in production of mechanical books. Immediately interested, Raphael Tuck turned to producing these books as well. Lothan Meggendorfer is considered by many to be the most creative producer of mechanical books between 1878 and 1819. In his creations one pull of a paper tab, set as many as three characters in motion simultaneously. In the space of these short years, he wrote and designed more than 300 mechanical books. World War I brought the importation of these to a halt. Publication of these books resumed in the 1920s, but British and American publishers could not resuscitate the postwar market. However, Czechoslovakia and Austria did produce single pop-up scenes to be used by parents to relate the tale of Santa Claus and his gift bearing. Today pop-up mechanical books are once again being manufactured, but never as artistically and creatively as in the past.

Closely related to these children's pop-up books are the pop-up type of nativity scenes which were used to adorn homes, classrooms, and churches. In addition to their decorative purposes, these were used to educate children in the story of Christ's birth. Ernst Kaufman of New York City created many of these in the early 1900s. Usually three-folded, these chromolithographed creche scenes provided a lavish three-dimensional image to their viewers.

A popular paper toy in the late 1800s was the panorama. This was a box with a window space in the center through which passed a series of colored pictures which had been lithographed on a long paper strip and wound around two wooden rollers situated at each end of the box. The child merely turned a small metal crank inserted in the top of one the rollers to start a fast-moving story into action. In the 1870s McLoughlin Brothers copyrighted a panorama entitled "Visit of Santa

Claus to the Happy Children." Also, at this time, in E. I. Horseman's illustrated catalog of toys for dealers, was a description of "Kriss Kringles's Christmas Tableaux." This was a moving diorama consisting of a theatre-like box with a window section similar to the panorama box construction, featuring small action cutouts of locomotives and ships, moved by means of hand-operated wires and strings. This was priced in the catalog at $1.50.

Mechanical toy book, early 1900s. $450-500

Pop-up scene, Czechoslovakia, mid-1930s. $145-160

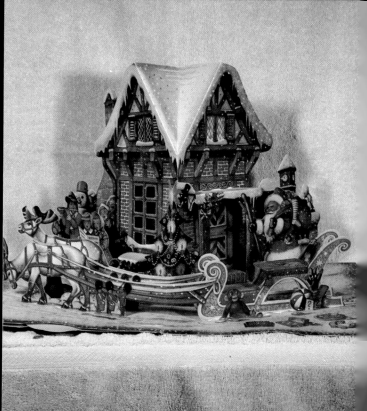

Early card booklet, late 1800s. $185-200

Chapter 5

GLASS ITALIAN ORNAMENTS

Italian figurals, early 1970s.
Left to right: $75-80, $40-45,
$40-45, $80-90.

Italian figurals, 1960s. Left, $90-1
Right, $100-110.

Although Italy had been exporting different items for sale at Christmas since 1947, it was not until 1952 that Italy began exporting to this country, very unique and unusual glass figural ornaments. Centered around the Lake Como region in Italy, these ornaments are blown in a number of small factories which have banded together to form a loose association. Dario Moranduzzo is the largest producer with the Bizzocchi, Brambilla, DeCarlini, Galvas, and Lemmi families also currently producing these figurals.

All these ornaments are handblown in the old manner, meaning, shaped by paddles as the glass bubble is slowly blown. It must be noted that the creation of these glass figurals is indeed an artistic achievement since these figurals are not blown from a mold. The process is somewhat similar to the process used by German glass blowers in the late 1800s. A glass tube which varies in size according to the size of the ornament being produced, is quickly heated and pulled by the artisan to create first the body then the head of the ornament. Then arms and legs are created by tiny tubes of glass attached at the appropriate spots after being heated. An experienced glassblower develops the ability to create an ornament in three to four minutes. Each of these has its own particular differences since no molds are used.

The manufacturing of Christmas ornaments does differ in Italy from other European countries in that each family does have its own factory for the production of their Christmas ornaments. All of the work is done in the factory unlike in Germany where much of it is still done in individual homes. Each Italian factory averages about forty employees of which only a few are the actual glassblowers. There are from ten to fifteen blowers in every large factory each with his own specialty. In addition, approximately ten artists are responsible for the individual painting and the addition of fabric and other trims. The painting is done by skilled artisans, carefully trained and cultivated. The resulting Italian ornaments are becoming increasingly collectible due to their individual artistic detail and creativity.

In 1955, Italy exported just over $22,000 worth of ornaments. Production of these ornaments has steadily increased each year with the exception of a lull when America experienced what is known in the trade as a "bad Christmas," due to the energy crisis and the consequent cut-back on the purchase of decorations. However, the market has since changed and current trends find these glass figurals to be among the most desirable of newer Christmas items due to their individual uniqueness and high quality. Today well over one million dollars in ornaments are exported by Italy each year.

There are several characteristics of Italian figurals which must be noted. The glass is extremely thin and fragile due to the extended legs, arms, and other such features. Stork's beaks and feet, as well as the arms and legs of other figures, are carefully drawn out into the thinnest of appendages. Thus, caution must be used in their use and storage. In addition, many of the first ornaments in the 1950s were trimmed with inexpensive materials such as feathers, cotton, pipe cleaners, maribou, and plush. These earlier ornaments deteriorate easily and caution must again be exercised in their storage. Collectors often ask about the determination of age. Silvering, coloring, and subject material are considerations of age. Bright, gaudy colors which are almost electric in nature along with inside silvering were used almost exclusively through the 1960s. The paint was applied quite heavily in vivid colors. Detail was good, but not as exact as might be expected. In the 1970s, unsilvered muted colored figurals became the most common. Most often ornaments were dipped in a single soft pastel color and

Painted by Maria Luisa de Carlini. $80-90

3-dimensional Italian ornaments, 1960s. $25-30 ea.

hen details added with black and other dark colored paints. Today more unsilvered than silvered figurals are being imported. Even though Italian figurals are fairly recent, subject material does help. Since cartoon characters and other popular personalities are again an indication of American interest, they were made only when these subjects were popular. Therefore, Charlie Brown, the Beatles, the Pink Panther, and other such subjects help to pin down a particular time frame.

Among the most rare of Italian figurals to first be imported into the United States was a set of Peter Pan related figurals including Peter Pan, Captain Hook, and an alligator with a clock painted on his belly. In 1955 a set of Italian figurals reached this country which included a ballerina with net skirt, an ice skater with cotton trim around neck and skirt, a skier complete with thin wooden skis, and a doll complete with cotton hair. The set sold for $2.98 and started an unbelievable variety of different figurals sold through the years. At first, such figurals were sold primarily by the set. It wasn't until the late 1960s that individual ornaments began to be sold by department and gift stores. Ironically much of their rarity is found in their creativity since they are handblown and were sold individually only in fine gift shops and department stores. Each of these was much more expensive and thus the quantity is quite low in comparison to other European imported glass Christmas tree ornaments.

The Italians, like the Germans, created figures representing different American personalities and interests. Among the most unique are the cartoon characters such as Donald Duck and Mickey Mouse as well as a complete set of the Beatles manufactured when the rock group was at the height of its popularity. Soldiers, snowmen, cowboys, and even a Statue of Liberty are represented in some of the different figurals blown. Since the 1970s, the Italians have especially capitalized on appealing to America's youth and the majority created since then are of animals, fairytale personalities, and cartoon characters.

The future of these Italian figurals is at this point quite uncertain, as many of the glassblowers themselves are in their 50s and 60s. Few young Italians are interested in continuing in their parents' glassblowing occupations with other professions appearing much more lucrative.

Their future rarity also is directly dependent upon the price which is high today in comparison to other possible ornaments. Even though the Italian figurals might appear more prominent today to collectors, it must not be forgotten that the Italians have become quite famous for their hand painted spheres and teardrop shaped ornaments. Maria Luisa De Carlini has for a great number of years hand painted a variety of ornaments for Bronner's of Michigan, as well as for a few other importers. Maria Luisa is especially known for her religious themes. Undoubtedly she would have continued to add much to the artistic line of Carlini had she not died at an early age from cancer in the 1970s. Presently Bronner's artist-in-residence, Connie V. Larson sketches a particular scene for an ornament, creates an ink drawing, films it, and then sends it to Italy with the exact specifications so Italian artists can hand paint each screen designed for an ornament.

Not quite as elaborate, but quite beautiful are the 3-D ornaments produced in Italy during the early through the mid-1960s. These ornaments were silvered indents with a concave interior flashed a bright blue or red. Glued to the concave indent were plastic molded designs including a nativity scene, a Santa, angel, snowman, church, and a house. These plastic scenes were painted in good detail. In addition to these, countless other Italian manufactured glass ornaments provided much glitter and creativity for America's Christmas trees.

Space figurals, early 1970s. Top: $140-150, $170-180. Bottom: $130-145.

Italian figurals, early 1970s. Top: $70-80, $60-70, $100-110. Bottom: $120-130, $140-150.

Italian figurals 1960s. Top: 160-175, $50-60, $75-80, $110-120. Middle: $80-90, $100-110, $85-95, $90-100. Bottom: $90-100, $80-90, $110-120, $70-80.

Italian figurals, early 1980s. Top: $160-170, $60-70, $95-110, $100-110. Middle: $110-120, $130-140, $100-110, $200-225. Bottom: $120-130, $130-140, $140-150.

Italian figurals, 1950s and 1960s. Top: $35-45, $55-65, $35-45, $75-85. Middle: $160-175, $80-90. Bottom: $185-200, $75-80, $145-155, $110-120, $65-75.

*Italian figurals, 1960s and early 1970s. Top: $50-60, $55-65, $70-80.
Middle: $25-30, $25-30, $15-20. Bottom: $20-25, $40-45, $25-35.*

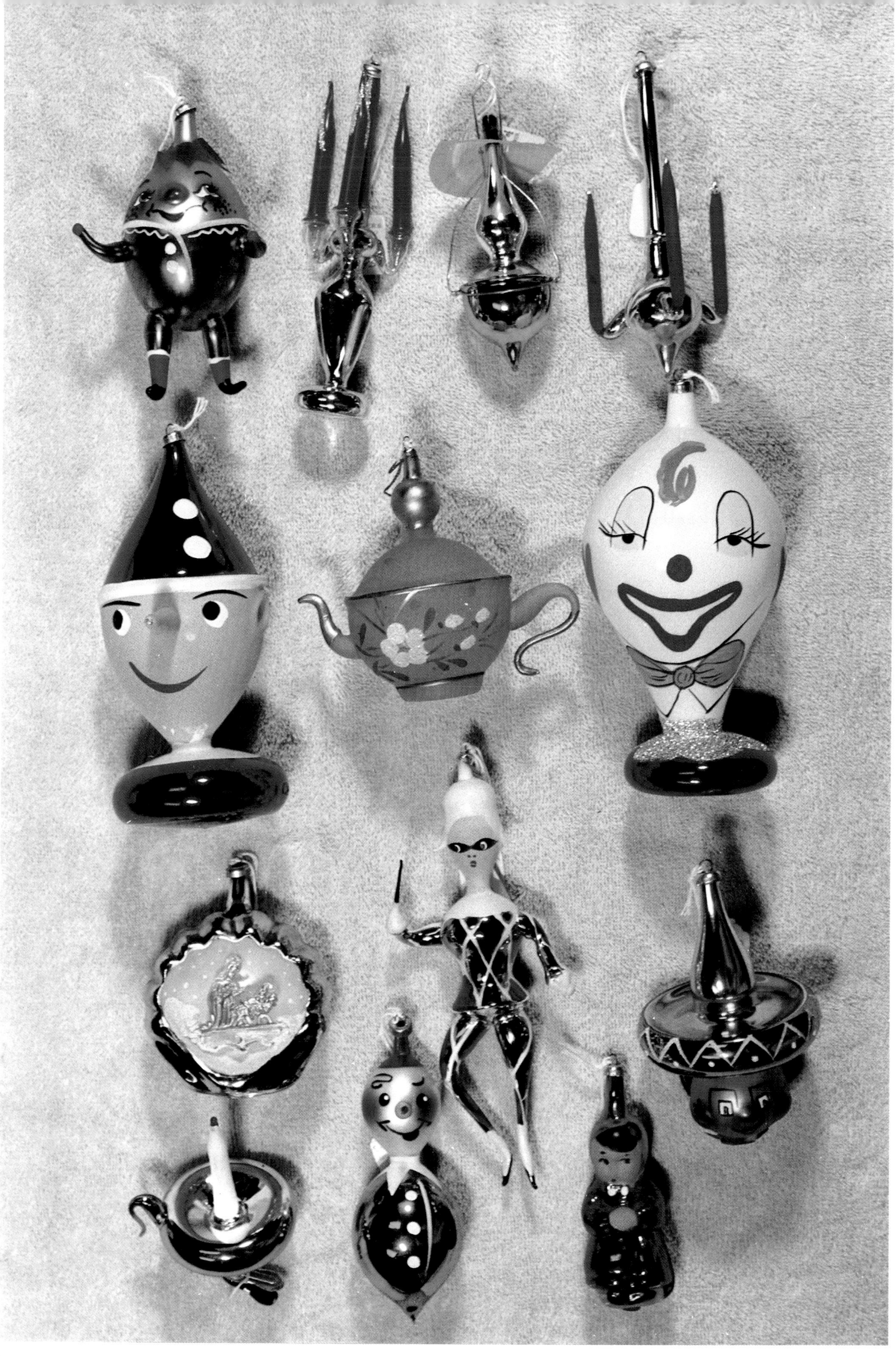

Opposite page: Italian figurals, 1970s and early 1980s. 1st row: $110-120, $95-100, $100-125, $110-120. 2nd row: $150-165, $50-60, $75-85. 3rd row: $50-60, $110-120, $90-100. 4th row: $75-85, $80-90, $40-45.

Italian figurals, 1950s and early 1960s. Top: $110-120, $140-160, $100-125, $110-120. Middle: $85-95, $90-100, $100-110, $95-110. Bottom: $150-200, $160-175, $110-120, $185-200.

Italian figurals, early 1970s. 1st row: $75-85, $110-115, $140-160, $175-185. 2nd row: $95-110, $100-110. 3rd row: $75-85, $120-130, $90-100. 4th row: $95-110, $95-110, $210-230.

Chapter 6

UNEXPLORED CATEGORIES
OF GLASS ORNAMENTS

Christmas Tree Toppers

Even though we pay a great deal of attention to the tops of our trees today, that was not the case in earlier times. Often it was not set off at all and occasionally just marked with a candle. During the 19th century, it was far more common to find the top decorated with tinsel flags, rosettes, angels, and stars.

In the 1870s, the star was initially made of plain gold foil; it was also made of crinkled wires, tinsel, sheet brass, or glass. In 1901 a price list offered three different stars for sale. There was a tinsel star with a smooth circle of stars and an angel picture in the center, a silver glass star with rich tinsel decoration and a spiral for fastening to the tree top, and a colored glass beaded star with a center of crinkled tinsel with a wire spiral spring for fastening. For a long period of time, the star remained as a symbol of the star of Bethlehem on many trees.

Some regions had their own way to adorn the tops of their trees. In the Palantinate, for instance, in the second half of the 19th century, "a rooster usually was displayed at the top, as on Protestant church steeples (2)." As a child, the author Bogumil Goltz saw "a golden apple at the top of the tree" when he experienced an old-Prussian Christmas at the house of his grandparents in 1808. In Frankonia the tree top was decorated by either an egg-sugar horseman or a gold foil angel.

This *Nuremberg* gold foil angel acquired supra-regional significance. At the time of the flowering Christmas branches which had no "top," it hung in the center. An early etching, *The Distribution of Christmas Gifts or The Merry Morning* by Joseph Keller (Nuremberg, 1770), illustrates a large angel, standing in a wreath and holding a candle in each of his outstretched hands as the central figure of the Christmas bush. As a result, the wax angel ornament surrounded by a circular goose feather branch is not all that unusual of an ornament as it is most likely an outgrowth of this particular custom. Early illustrations of Christmas fairs from the beginning of the 19th century show tall, stern angels with spread arms at the tops of the firs or pines. Typically all had a high, straight cap or crown on short hair, a stiff shirt front, or a ribbon placed around the neck and crossed at the waist. The feet are usually visible under the long skirt. The later Nuremberg gold foil angel, as we generally know it, has no arms and no legs; he wears a wide

scapulary with fringes of gold foil, a full pleated skirt of gold paper with a pinafore over it, and a crown low on his forehead.

According to legend, a Nuremberg doll maker made the first gold foil angel after the 30-years War in memory of his little daughter Anna, who had died. Regardless of legend, it is certain that the manufacture of gold foil angels is based on the Nuremberg tradition of doll-making and on the toy industry of neighboring Sonneberg, whose wares were sold in Nuremberg. Brass foundries, which produced very thin, loudly rustling sheet brass, were situated in the area around Nuremberg. Following developments in the doll industry the gold foil angel, which initially had a shoulder head of wax or papier-mâché, with wooden lower legs and arms, was given a shoulder head, and arms and legs of bisque during the second half of the 19th century.

Occasionally, there would be a rosy cherub, dressed in only a diaper, at the top of the tree. Today this is the larger type wax or waxed angel with spun glass wings that is found by collectors. Later angels had a skirt trimmed in lace and decorated with ribbons and tinsel thread.

With the popularity of "scrap" ornaments in the late 1800s, came the use of embossed and die-cut chromolithographs as "top" ornaments for the Christmas tree. For the top, one usually used angels with a book or scroll proclaiming, "Peace on Earth" or "Gloria in excelsis deo." Elaborate, large, chromolithographs were especially fashioned for floor to ceiling Victorian parlor trees. They were usually transferred onto cardboard, glued onto gold stars, or surrounded by tinsel.

There were also metal angels for the top, finished in several colors, 4 3/4" to 8" tall. Fashioned from thin tin, they were deeply embossed and detailed. These metal angels are of the same type as those used for the revolving tree tops employing chimes and candles. Revolving tree tops were extremely popular from the late 1800s, continuing into the 1920s. The first metal revolving tree tops employed four candles. After the candles were lit, the chimes sound in three harmoniously tuned keys, resembling church bells heard from a distance. With the advent of electric lights, an electrically lit metal tree top quite similar to the candle-lit one was offered for sale in the mid-1920s into 1932. It was a combination top with a motor used to revolve the upper part and a light socket in the very top which held a C-6 light.

The glass Christmas tree toppers, whose basic shape is reminiscent of the Prussian spiked helmet, had not come on the market until

Early paper and glass top, ca. 1910. $250-275

American composition angel, 1940s. $150-165

Manitowoc tinsel angel top, late 1940s. $50-95

American tree tops, 1940s and 1950s. $20-50 ea.

Tinsel tree tops, early 1920s. $90-130 ea.

German tree tops, 1920s and 1930s. $80-90 ea.

Elaborate glass angel, 1930s. $600-650

American made tree tops, 1950s. Left to right: $80-90, $65-75, $80-90.

the end of the 19th century, but their popularity quickly caused the disappearance of the angels, rosettes, and stars.

In 1913 Sears Roebuck advertised a tree top with a large ball entirely wrapped in crinkly wire with a pointed top crowned by tinsel sprays. This type of top became quite popular with elaborate ones wire-wrapped with as many as five spheres (often indented) and embellished on the sides with tiers of tiny glass bells with glass clappers that were sure to ring in the drafty parlors of yesteryear. Sears continued to offer wire-wrapped tree tops for sale until imports were cut off by World War I. Before World War I, large 6 1/2" silvered stars of Bethlehem were sold for the price of 15 cents.

Starting in the mid-1920s, a popular tree top ornament became the silver colored tinsel sprays decorated with glass balls at the end of each spray. Selling for no more than 40 cents, these were put on the top of the tree by a nail. These tinsel tops continued to be popular until after the Depression in this country, replacing the intricate glass tops used previously. They were popular since they were unbreakable and did not contain the glass tube which so often shattered when they were put on top of the tree.

It was not until the 1930s that glass tops were once again in fashion, this time appearing with stronger bottoms which broke less frequently. It is during this period of time that many of the elaborate reflector sphered tops were made. These were often as high as 18" and employed a series of exquisite spheres.

In 1935 Lauschan glass blowers supplied the latest novelty glass ornaments. They were hand-blown, 5 1/2" silvered angels, floating on a cloud of spun glass, equipped with gold wings and silk belts, to keep them in a floating position. Other forms were, a standing angel and Santa Claus blown of glass, realistically painted, and perched on a cloud of curled spun glass. These large, elaborate, thin-blown figural tree tops are among the most rare today commanding extremely high prices. Paper crowns and other foil trim were abundantly used. These continued to be manufactured up to World War II.

During this period of time, most tree tops were identified by a paper label reading, "Made In Germany" or simply "Germany." In the early 1930s a plain white label with black printing was used. The blue and white printed label came into use in the mid-1930s and continued until exports were cut off with the start of World War II. It was during the late 1930s that Corning, Premier Glass, and Shiny Brite produced American made tree tops. All of these were of heavy glass and very few of them contained reflector spheres. The colors were two toned or monochromatically designed with bright pinks, blues, and reds being predominate.

Several more recently manufactured tree tops continue to confuse collectors. One example is that of a chromolithographed angel with foil wings emerging from a cloud of curled spun glass completely circled by spun glass and gold foil stars. This top was made in the 1940s by National Tinsel of Manitowoc, Wisconsin, and was completely manufactured in this country. Also, a papier-mâché kneeling angel with silver crown and wings, often thought to be much earlier, is actually an American product of the 1940s. Another angel top that was manufactured in the United States during the 1950s is the satin skirted angel with braided hair and a gold crown. This particular angel has a composition face over a silvered paper cone. A later variety of this was constructed entirely of plastic, with a light bulb illuminating the entire decoration. Plastic also provided a Santa tree top with a C-7 bulb which appeared on thousands of American trees between 1954 and 1958. Most of the plastic tree tops did not survive since the intense heat of the bulb would crack and shattered many of this not so durable plastic.

Within the last five years tree tops have once again gained true artistry and creativity with many elaborate glass tops being imported from West Germany, East Germany, and Italy. The star theme has been re-introduced by Bronner's with Italian manufactured glass stars identical to those first made at the turn of the century. There are many who feel only experienced European glass blowers can handle the intricacies of producing such decorations. The only imports handled by Shiny Brite today are tree top ornaments which are difficult to make and have long been an old European specialty. Coby Glass is the only American company to produce tree top ornaments domestically today.

Glass Beads and Glass Beaded Garlands

Some of the most desirable of glass decorations at the present time are the old fashioned beaded ornaments and glass strands of beads that festooned trees of years ago. Today these beads are extremely rare and it is becoming increasingly difficult for collectors to amass enough beading to decorate an entire tree.

Glass beads were among the first glass items produced in Lauscha. Bead blowing grew out of the need to give the people of Lauscha the ability to process glass house products in a small workshop "at the lamp." It was probably in the second half of the 18th century that the manufacturing of beads was begun in Lauscha under favorable conditions. With the so-called "boot pipe" (a winding pipe) one blew through a rape oil flame (later paraffin was used) and thus created a primitive jet of flame. Within the flame one heated a glass rod, produced by a glass house, quickly exchanged the "boot pipe" for the glass rod and blew the heated spot into a ball-shape. Later the use of a bellows (the so-called goat-bag), squeezed under one arm, made this job easier.

In the second phase of work, the beads were separated from the rod and silvered with lead or fish-silver, then filed with wax. For a long time they were the main source of income for the lamp-blowers of Thuringia.

Finally, the production of larger ball-shaped Christmas tree ornaments, as we know them today, began. At this same time, in Glabonz, there was also an independent manufacturing of beaded ornaments quite unrelated to what was occurring in Lauscha. The first glass-house in Glabonz (in what was then Bohemia) was established in 1845. Small glass beads were blown as in Thuringia, but mainly thin glass tubes and solid rods were processed by cutting and pressing. At the polishing wheel, the blowers would break off little pieces of glass, about 3/4" to 1 1/4" long, so-called "bits," or hacked apart round glass tubes with a "guillotine." The home workers of Glabonz combined these pieces with hollow glass beads which had been blown freehand or in faceted molds. With leonic wires or string they made differently shaped ornaments as well as beaded chains for use on the tree. It seems very likely that the intricate strings of blown beads which contain rods of colored glass are products of Glabonz rather than of Lauscha and the surrounding German villages. The chains of blown beads and pear-shaped ornaments, both freeblown and molded appear to be products of Germany.

Even though larger ornaments gained more attention due to their popularity and ease in blowing, the manufacturing of small beads as Christmas tree decorations was firmly established for a period of time. Perhaps many younger blowers learned their trade through the manufacturing of these tiny beads.

Part of the rarity of these beads lies in the fact that the manufacturing process was so long due to the great amount of time needed to produce a single strand of eight to ten beads, the first popular form of sales. These strands were first used to fill in empty spots characteristic of the old-fashioned unsheared trees. Later in the early 1900s, beads were sold in up to 75" lengths for festooning the tree. These long beaded chains continued to be sold over the years, becoming less intricate and creative with the passage of time. Eventually Japan became the principal producer of glass garland beads.

Often collectors are amazed at the variety of shapes found beaded together on a single strand. The most common chains are those of evenly shaped round beads whereas the most rare are those containing different molded beads and spheres. Occasionally beads were unsilvered and finished with soft pastel paint. The most precious of these were individually wrapped before World War I with thin silver crinkly wire. In 1913, Sears Roebuck advertised beads with fine silvered tinsel, making it hard to break the glass. Crinkly wire, as well as being beautiful, was quite functional since it helped prevent damage while being shipped as well as when in use by the consumer. Ten strings with ten beads to each string were sold for 79 cents. That same year, satin finished beads between ovals 16" in length were offered with again ten per assortment. Rarity is also determined by size, for some beads are up to 2" in diameter and were blown for large Victorian floor to ceiling trees. Single beads were sold in quantities so that individuals could create their own artistic shapes and color schemes. In addition, many of the strings broke over the years which caused previous decorators to combine beads in whatever fashion was necessary to finish decorating the tree. Since the earlier beads are very thin and fragile, they were easily broken and had to be removed from many chains, again causing additional variations.

The most common chains have beads of a uniform size. After World War I, Sears Roebuck offered beads for sale 1/2" in diameter with ten beads per string. Blues, reds, and greens were sandwiched in between gold and silver beads in a simple color design. Round beads in solid colors, set off by different colored striped beads were also offered for sale for 75 cents. All of the beads after World War I were heavier in weight so there would be less breakage. German manufactured chains can be identified by thin paper circular disks at the ends of each chain to contain the beads. Further indications of German beads are fine muted colors, thin glass used before World War I, and worn silvering. These silvered beads quickly deteriorated inside due to the amount of air which entered at both sides of the beads.

Heavier glass beads were produced by Japan starting in the early 1930s and continued to be made through the 1960s. Earlier Japanese strings contained different color combinations and sizes whereas those made in the 1960s contained the same size and color of beads. Common colors were bright red, green, gold, blue, and silver. All the beads were marked with a paper label indicating Japan as the manufacturer. If this is missing, collectors should look for a star shaped paper disk found at the end. When plain uncolored stars are used it is from before World War II for it appears that foil stars were used in the '50s and '60s at both ends of each individual chain.

The storage of such chains is very important since collectors will need to carefully layer these beads so they will not become entangled and broken.

(2) Bogumil Golta: *Ein Jugendleben.* Leipzig 1852, page 74.

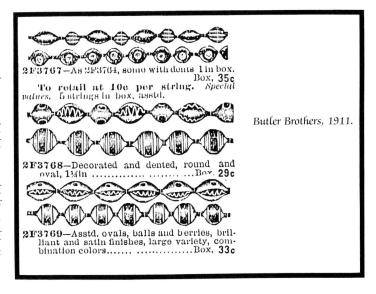

Butler Brothers, 1911.

81

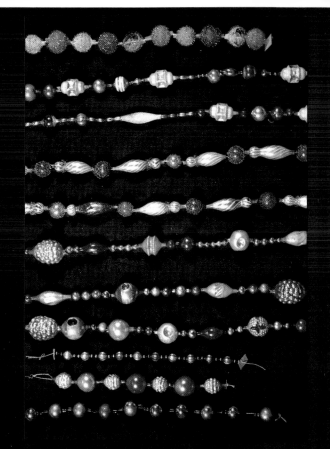
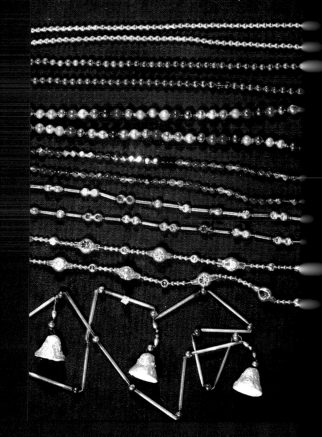

Art glass animals, late 1920s. Left to right: $80-90; $165-180; $90-100.

Animals and favor vases, early 1920s. Left to right: $80-90; $130-210; $190-220; $100-110.

Fighting roosters, early 1930s. $230-250.

Collectors often question the age and history of hollow heavy glass figural decorations which are found as tree ornaments or as free-standing table decorations. These figures are made of milk glass or colored glass which is silvered internally or occasionally, left unsilvered. It seems that the majority of these figurals are animals. In the first decades of this century, hollow glass animals, which usually stood as knick-knacks in curio cabinets, had their beginnings as Christmas tree ornaments with melted on hangers or metal clips.

The earliest of these figurals appear to be those of the milk glass variety. Many of these free-standing animals were deer posed with a small vase attached to a clear rectangular base. Most historians feel these free standing decorations were really, for all practical purposes, "place settings" for dinner parties during the Christmas season. Name cards were placed between the animal and the vase, which was designed to contain a tiny nosegay of flowers or Christmas greenery. These particular deer were made in Steinhold as early as 1870, although it appears that the majority of those found by collectors today are from the early 1920s. The combination of milk glass with pastel and clear glass is characteristic of this period. Milk glass animals are prized for their exquisite detail and free blown forms. Each animal is individually blown like Italian figurals today. Although the majority found today are deer, the Germans also did creae milk glass pigs, chicks, roosters, and probably other farm animals as well.

Appearing in the mid-1920s, were silvered animals and birds of all varieties to be used as tree ornaments. Constructed of clear or colored glass, literally hundreds of hand blown birds and animals were produced. Storks, ducks, penguins, elephants, horses, and other figures were blown usually from the blue glass during this period of time and had a small paper label reading, "Germany" with a star in the center. Small detailed feet made from opaque orange colored glass were added with small black dots for eyes. In the early 1930s, animals made from clear glass and silvered inside became extremely fashionable and thousands of tall-legged elegant storks were created. Ranging in size from fourteen inches to three inches in height, these storks had long elegant orange feet and beaks. With graceful curved necks and tails, these free-standing birds were sold in sets of three and were table decorations year around. In fact, so many were lovingly placed in curio cabinets, that third generation owners have forgotten that these were first intended as Christmas table decorations. Also found are clear glass figures encased with ribbons of rainbow colors. Silvered inside, such animals with annealed hooks are the rarest form of art glass ornaments. All ornaments of this type, produced in the 1930s until the start of World War I, were marked with a blue and white paper label reading, "Made in Germany."

Variations of this type of art glass are seen in the multitudes of table decorations intended for use during different seasons of the year. The variety seems endless as sleighs containing Santa pulled by tiny glass reindeer are found along with Art Deco types of human figures and animals. What fascinates collectors most about these table decorations are the free flow of lines and the endless variety of subject material. Even realistically painted glass fruit have been discovered. This is one area that definitely will see collecting growth.

The "iciclet" types of Art Glass ornaments are another variety which became very popular starting in the mid-1930s. These are not as early as originally thought by Christmas historians. They are usually not hollow blown, but are twisted of solid glass "wire," have melted-on hooks, and at the bottom taper off to a point. Some of them were manufactured with complex twists and occasionally several of them were melted together. Probably an outgrowth of the clear glass icicle, these ornaments quickly became extremely creative with thin Santa Clauses and indents fused to twisted glass "wires" that would encircle the inside figure. Not many were hand blown due to the fact that they were extremely delicate and their thin clear glass easily broke.

Using a similar technique, a Lauscha glass blower of the 1930s created small frames of clear glass and threaded glass with melted-on hangers for the Christmas tree. Into these glass hoops he melted colored glass toys like animals, trees, birds, chimney sweeps, and a multitude of other items. Also quite rare due to the individual time needed to complete such ornaments, these will be counted among the most rare of German glass ornaments in years to come.

Kugels and Other Bras-Capped Ornaments

Among the most fascinating are those early, heavy glass ornaments which were the first glass decorations for the Christmas tree. *Christmas Past* outlines their manufacturing technique as well as an early history of their gradual development into the thin glass figurals so loved by millions of Christmas enthusiasts. *Harrap's Standard German-English Dictionary* defines "kugel" as a sphere or ball and even uses the illustrative example, "den Weinachtsbaum mit bunten kugeln behangen" which translates to "to decorate the Christmas tree with brightly colored balls." It is true, then, if one is to take this definition literally, that only the round ornaments may be called "kugels." However, in that case, this term would apply to all round Christmas ornaments, including the modern spring cap hanging Shiny Brites.

What are the traits which set "kugels" apart from other Christmas ornaments? They are usually heavy glass. There is also a variety of lighter glass brass- capped ornaments often referred to as "kugel-likes." These are not of Japanese manufacture, but are either American or European, because the beautiful amethyst color with the iridescent sheen is found in both kugels and kugel-likes. It is also occasionally found in very old bead chains of European origin. This color has never been characteristic of Japanese ornaments. "Trimming the Christmas Tree at Both Ends of the Nineteen Century," an article devoted to Christmas decorations, includes pictures of the kugel-likes which imitate the shape of the European sugar plums. These sugar plums have the same brass caps as all the other light weight "kugel-likes." All Japanese ornaments which have hangers similar to the kugel-likes have plain silver colored caps and rings and the design in the glass is much less carefully molded. It is likely that the brass-capped kugel-likes represent a transitional phase between the heavy glass kugels and the modern balls with the two piece spring cap hangers.

An additional characteristic of kugels is that the majority have a brass cap and ring for hanging. Also most of them come in one of three different shapes. By far, the most common are the balls; grapes are second; and the egg shapes, more commonly referred to as pear-shaped, are third.

Kugels vary as to color, size, thickness of glass, shape, silvering, and caping. Almost all heavy glass ornaments, as far west as Wisconsin, come in the four most common colors: silver, gold, green, and cobalt blue. The blue ones tend to be slightly less plentiful, and consequently, higher in price than the others. The red kugels are considered quite uncommon, and the amethyst are outright rare. Besides these, there are a few unusual colors such as bronze and aqua which are seldom seen. With most kugels, the color is in the glass, except for the silver ones which get their color from the coating inside the ornament. Some of them are also decorated with paint on the surface as well. There does exist a silver ball which has horizontal bronze, purple, and aqua stripes; a silver bunch of grapes with pink touches on the fruit;

and a large silver kugel with small blue six-pointed stars on it. Painted kugels are not common, and perhaps some of these painted designs are later additions. Almost all kugels are silvered inside.

There is a great deal of variation in the size of kugels. The largest seems to be fourteen inches in diameter. These were hung from the ceiling rather than on the Christmas tree. Most of the smaller ornaments are three-quarters of an inch in size. Since the balls, particularly, were hand blown, one sometimes finds two balls of exactly the same diameter which are very different in weight due to the variations in thickness of the glass.

One of the most interesting distinguishing features of kugels are their caps. A few of the oldest have blown glass hanging devices or corks in the opening and are hung from wires or hooks which extend into the cork. The majority have brass caps and rings. The cap may be combined with a cork which is inserted into the opening, or they simply have wires bent outward inside the kugel, keeping the cap in place. One can often spot this type of hanging device, for if the cap is at all loose, the ends of the wire move and rub the silver off from inside the ornament, resulting in a noticeable ring, somewhat below the cap. The designs on the caps are often quite beautiful. The four which are the most common, for want of better names, can be termed as (1) Eight-Petal Design [On the really large kugels, this same design is expanded to ten petals.]; (2) Baroque Design; (3) Five Leaf Design; and (4) Swirl-Leaf and Rim Design.

Common Cap Designs:

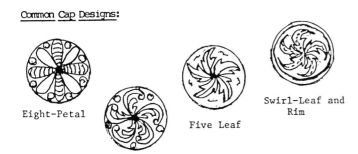

Eight-Petal Baroque Five Leaf Swirl-Leaf and Rim

About ninety percent of the spheres seem to have one of these four types of caps. All of the heavy glass grapes have either Eight-Petal, Baroque, or Five Leaf caps, and the pear shapes most often have Eight-Petal caps. However, one exception was found which has an unusual design on the cap. Illustrated below are the less common caps found on kugels.

Less Common Cap Designs:

Glass kugel-like grapes were made by the American glass blower, William A. DeMuth and several German immigrant glass blowers living in New York and New Jersey. These heavy glass grapes had several variations in form. There is a very regular conical shape, a more irregular shape with mold lines which show it was made in a three-part mold, and a more unusual form which includes leaves in the mold. The earliest of glass grapes featured a prominent central vein on the ornament which twisted and curled about, eventually forming a hanger from which to attach the ornament. According to Maggie Rogers, author of *The Glass Christmas Tree Ornament*, these were made about 1830-1840 for use as decorative pieces. By the 1880s both pear and grape ornaments were topped with an embossed cap which supported a brass ring for hanging. No doubt these early glass grapes were blown in the United States rather than in Europe as originally thought. Some other unusual shapes include apples, ovoid shapes with three indents, berries, ridged spheres, and pear shapes. It appears very possible that other fruit shapes will eventually be found. The lighter weight "kugel-likes" come in a greater variety of shapes, but there is less variation in the cap. Almost all have a rather plain common cap.

There are many more shapes in these lighter weight ornaments. Examples of shapes in my collection are:

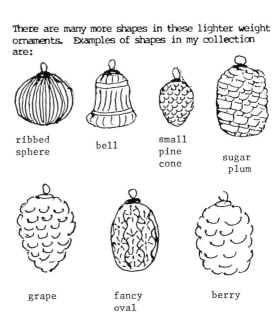

ribbed sphere bell small pine cone sugar plum

grape fancy oval berry

There are many more shapes in these lighter weight ornaments. Examples of shapes which have been discovered by collectors include:

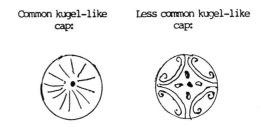

Common kugel-like cap: Less common kugel-like cap:

Besides the traditional kugel colors, kugel-likes also come in white milk glass. Pine cones and sugar plums have been found in such milk glass. It is obvious that kugels and kugel-likes are not as simple as they might appear, for there are many different variations available for collectors to find in addition to the very common spheres. Only with continued collecting will this category become more complete historically.

Chapter 7

NATIVITY SCENES CELEBRATING THE BIRTH OF CHRIST

Elaborate fold-out crèche, late 1800s. $200-225

Intricate fold-out, late 1880s. $250-275

Detailed fold-out, early 1900s. $300-325

3-dimensional crèche, German, 1920s. $110-130

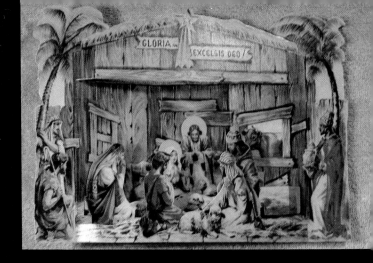

3-dimensional crèche, American, 1940s. $50-60

Composition crèche, 1898. $100-125

Clemco musical crèche, mid-1950s. $80-100

It has been a tradition in many families to build under the tree or on a small table, a descriptive scene re-enacting the birth of Christ. For the benefit of collectors, it may be useful to first explore a few descriptive terms used to describe this scene. The French term *Creche* is used in America as well as in France. In England, Italy, and German-speaking countries, the direct translation of *manger* is used, hence *crib*, *prescepio*, or *krippe*, respectively. In Spain and Latin America, the term Santos covers shrine and crib figures. The Christ Child alone carries the international term of *Bambino*. At one time, this "devotional toy" or "amusement of the rich" was the hobby of the aristocracy and royalty. It was also the "passion" of the Pennsylvania Germans who dedicated weeks of work to constructing a *Putz* scene, the center of which was the Christmas crib. Where collectors can point to Germany as the birthplace of the Christmas decoration industry, they can look to Italy for the birthplace of the Nativity scene.

One of the important contributions by Italy to the Christmas season were creche scenes and figurines. These are, of course, based on the re-enactment of the birth of Christ by St. Francis of Assisi, and an artistic friend named Giovanni Velita. Dating back to the 18th century, artisans in Naples produced terra-cotta headed puppet-like figures, elaborately dressed and outfitted. At their beginning, these cribs were limited to a few figures. Gradually these creches came to include scenes like the flight into Egypt, the nuptials at Cana of Galilee, Jesus among the scribes, and other such striking incidents. Human figures, like peasants, fishermen, beggars, and soldiers, mingled with well known characters of the Bible. Most of those made in Italy were of wax or terra-cotta. The making of these figures opened a large field to the wood-carver when the custom spread to the Tyrol and southern Germany. A fine specimen of a complete Christmas crib carved from wood may be seen at Oberammergau. The first figures purchased were of the Holy Family and others were added over the years. In 1911, Maximilian Krausz, writing of the Munich market in *Moderne Kunst*, describes the children wandering about among the long rows of booths searching for creche figures. At this Munich market, separate parts of the wax figures were available: hands, feet, or heads, as well as individual figures, animals, palms, and cypresses. The Bavarian museum in Munich has a splendid collection of cribs gathered from all parts of the country which is considered today to be among its most valuable treasures. Most Neapolitan creches and early wax and wood German-made figures are museum pieces and they elude most collectors.

Many creche scenes found today in the United States are an outgrowth of "Putz scenes" so very popular among the Moravians in Pennsylvania. In *Ladies Home Journal*, Theodocia Walton in December, 1926, explicitly describes this Pennsylvania Christmas custom. She refers to the Christmas "Putz" by its German name, "Die Weihnachtskrippe," or the "Manger Crib of the Savior." She suggested that if one wished to duplicate such a scene, certain steps were to be taken. In late November or early December, one ought to gather fern moss and keep it in damp burlap bags. A week before Christmas, one should create a platform of old boxes or crates. Behind these crates, place small three to five foot Christmas trees, kept fresh in cans, filled with water and lumps of coal to steady them. Cover the platform with firewood, then burlap bags or heavy cloths, and then the moss. This will create an uneven ground and irregularity, essential to natural beauty. At the back, build mountains of rock paper.

Rare glass enclosed crèche, late 1800s. $650-700

Select the proper spot for the stable, and above it hang the star that guided the shepherds. Then it is up to the individual creator to add buildings, smaller brush or paper trees, animals, and human figurines to complete the setting. A pond, made of a small mirror or pan filled with water is a further possibility for more creativity. Since there is such a "creative license" involved here, it would not be unusual to find a tiger lurking behind a tree or a zebra peeking in the stable adoring the Christ Child. Candles were used for years, stuck in the moss for beauty, until the advent of electric lights. As modern toys were created, it became common to find, in these *Putz* scenes, electric trains circling the hills and valleys or windmills electrically turning their sails underneath the Christmas tree.

As a focal point of the "Putz" scene, the Christmas crib was an important item to purchase for many families. Depending upon their financial circumstances, they could purchase hand-carved, bisque, composition, plaster, cardboard, or paper figures in a large variety of sizes. Among the most expensive were the hand-carved creche figures from Erzgebirge. In this area of abundant wood, carvers have for years, been hand-carving various Nativity figures, leaving them natural or painting them in realistic detail. Bisque figures from noted ceramic manufacturers in Germany also were extremely expensive. The most affordable, and therefore, the easiest to find today, are those made of composition, plaster, cardboard, and paper.

Composition and plaster figures were molded in abundance with the most beautifully detailed figures available in the 1920s and early 1930s. The manufacturing of these is like the process of creating Santa figures which is covered in Chapter 1. Some of the most elaborate creche scenes are those three-dimensional fold-outs done in a variety of sizes in both heavy cardboard and paper. The most elaborate styles date to before World War I. After the War, Germany did again create three-dimensional scenes, but they were simple, three to four layers deep, unlike the up to 24 deep layer type made before World War I. West Germany has continued to print and produce these paper scenes, but the quality of printing has greatly declined.

During and immediately after World War II, Nativity sets employing plastic figures were primarily manufactured in the United States. Some composition figured creches were sold. These sets lacked a great amount of quality with poorly defined figures and a minimum of paint detail. In 1956, Nativity sets which included Swiss music boxes and plastic figures, were sold by Montgomery Wards and Sears Roebuck. These plastic fronted fiberboard stables came complete with a green "grass" mat to use under the set. Manufactured in the United States, these sets sold from five to ten dollars each. One of the most unusual was a complete unit with a music box playing "Silent Night" and a wind-up circular platform creating a procession of wise men and shepherds. Manufactured by the Clemco Company, this set included a C-7 1/2 lamp and cord for electrification.

Beautiful Nativity sets with wood stables and plaster figures continued to be imported into the United States after World War II. These were still painted realistically with the most perfect of detail. However, the demand for such artistry was dwindling, and Germany soon lost its share of this market due to the influx of more inexpensive sets from Japan and Italy. Papier-mâché figures were primarily produced by Italy in the 1950s and 1960s with some figures as high as 10 1/2".

The 1970s continued to find most Nativity sets imported from Japan and Italy. The most notable point of this period was the commencement of polyvinyl chloride figures (plastic) which continued to enjoy a great amount of popularity due to its durability and strength. Today the American market still has available creche figures from Italy and Germany; however, Japan and Taiwan are the principal suppliers. Creche scenes are somewhat challenging to collect since complete sets in excellent condition are difficult to find for they were used for many years and most often, are kept in families and passed down from generation to generation.

Sears Roebuck, 1931.

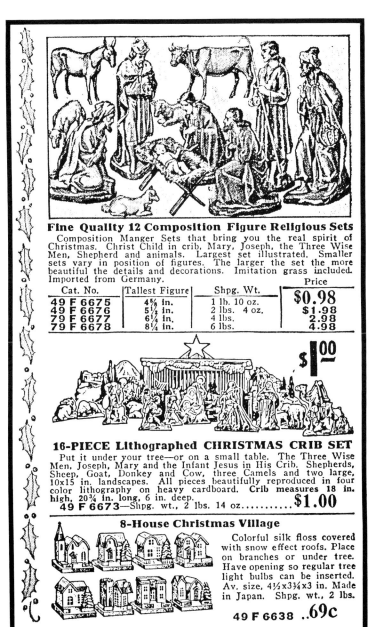

Fine Quality 12 Composition Figure Religious Sets
Composition Manger Sets that bring you the real spirit of Christmas. Christ Child in crib, Mary, Joseph, the Three Wise Men, Shepherd and animals. Largest set illustrated. Smaller sets vary in position of figures. The larger the set the more beautiful the details and decorations. Imitation grass included. Imported from Germany.

Cat. No.	Tallest Figure	Shpg. Wt.	Price
49 F 6675	4⅝ in.	1 lb. 10 oz.	$0.98
49 F 6676	5½ in.	2 lbs. 4 oz.	$1.98
79 F 6677	6¼ in.	4 lbs.	2.98
79 F 6678	8¼ in.	6 lbs.	4.98

16-PIECE Lithographed CHRISTMAS CRIB SET
Put it under your tree—or on a small table. The Three Wise Men, Joseph, Mary and the Infant Jesus in His Crib, Shepherds, Sheep, Goat, Donkey and Cow, three Camels and two large, 10x15 in. landscapes. All pieces beautifully reproduced in four color lithography on heavy cardboard. Crib measures 18 in. high, 20¾ in. long, 6 in. deep.
49 F 6673—Shpg. wt., 2 lbs. 14 oz.......... **$1.00**

8-House Christmas Village
Colorful silk floss covered with snow effect roofs. Place on branches or under tree. Have opening so regular tree light bulbs can be inserted. Av. size, 4½x3¾x3 in. Made in Japan. Shpg. wt., 2 lbs.
49 F 6638 ..69c

Sears Roebuck, 1934.

Imported Colorful Silk Floss Covered Christmas Villages

8 Buildings
These villages spread out under the tree or perched among the branches, or used with toy electric trains will give a most colorful effect. Insert a little bulb from your lighting outfit in small opening of house. When lit up, village lends real Christmas atmosphere. Roofs are sprinkled with glittering imitation snow which gives a sparkling effect when the light is on. Houses can be used as candy fillers as well. Two sizes. Small set illustrated.

Our Popular Priced Set	**Our De Luxe Set**
Average size overall 4x3¼x2¼ inches. Shpg. wt., 1¼ lbs. **89c**	Average size overall, 5½x3x4¼ inches. Shpg. wt., 2 lbs. **$1.49**
49F6637—8 houses......	49F6633—8 houses.

Chapter 8

SNOW BABIES AND BISQUE FIGURES

"Snowed" babies, early 1920s. Left to right: $130-150, $125-150, $110-130.

Santa figures in action, 1920s. Left to right: $100-110, $210-240, $100-125.

Bisque children without snow, 1920s. Left to right: $100-110, $100-110, $285-300, $100-110.

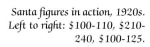

Japanese snow babies, 1930s. Left to right: $185-200, $300-325, $90-100.

German snow babies, 1920s. Left, $120-140; Right, $225-250.

Snow babies, German, 1920s. Left to right: $200-210, $200-230, $250-300, $400-425.

Bisque figures, Japanese, 1930s. Left to right: $100-110, $110-130, $110-120.

There is an extreme amount of disagreement between Christmas historians as to the origin of these so termed "Snow Babies" or "Sugar Dolls." One of the most widely accepted theories is that these tiny bisque figurines are the result of the birth of a girl, Marie Ahnighito Peary on September 12, 1893, to Admiral and Mrs. Peary of Greenland. Being the first white baby to grace that far northern land caused Eskimos to travel great distances to view the curiosity of such a white child.

Maria was named Ah-Poo-Mickaninny which translates into English as "Snow Baby" by the Eskimos and Annighito after the Eskimo woman who made the famous snowsuit which the Snow Baby always wore. Further support for this theory is strengthened by the fact that Mrs. Peary wrote *The Snow Baby* in 1901, followed by an equally successful second book in 1903 entitled, *Children of the Artic, by the Snow Baby and Her Mother.* In 1904, Mr. Peary wrote *Snowland Fold* and Maria published her own story in 1934, *The Snowbaby's Own Story.* The theory continues in that these tiny bisque dolls, found by collectors today, were created by German craftsmen as a commemoration of Maria's popularity.

Another theory is that the Snow Baby was a direct result of the Sugar Doll which was produced early in the 19th century, well before the birth of Maria Peary. Although the birth of the Peary child added to the popularity of the bisque dolls, some historians feel that the candy doll concoction of gum, tragacanth, flour, and sugar covered by an application of vegetable coloring definitely pre-dates Maria's birth.

These candy dolls called "tannenbaumkonfekt" in Germany were used as Christmas decorations in the early 1800s. Later, some were made of marzipan, a confection of crushed almonds, sugar, and egg whites. This eventually seems to have encouraged Johann Moll of Lubeck, Germany, to commission Hertwig and Company to create Snow Dolls from hand-whipped bisque later covered by grout.

Regardless of the historical origin, Snow Babies flooded the American market and became popular Christmas decoration items. These bisque figurines can be divided into either "snow" or "no snow" as well as into single and group settings. "Snow" figures have a pebbled rough exterior which resembles fallen snow. "No snow" figures have a smooth painted surface. "No snows" were made prior to World War I. B. Shackman and Co., New York, imported both "snow" and "no snow" and used them as illustrations in various catalogs. The rarer groupings employ both finishes.

Collectors consider the single figures in action poses to be quite rare also, along with the jointed Snow Babies with movable arms and legs. Snow Babies on top of candy containers and pincushions can be included with this group. Most common are the standing single figures. Action group poses include a mother pushing two babies in a buggy, a snow baby in a sleigh pulled by two husky dogs, and a baby on an airplane. Santas, snowmen, and animals such as polar bears, dogs, and deer were also popular subject material in this category. Single figures include falling children, skaters, sledders, and skiers. Galluba and Hoffman made the blue-gray snow children which were marked with a Shield (inside of which is an intertwined scripted G and H) topped by a crossed crown. Underneath the crown in capital letters is "Germany." Hertwig & Company and Heber & Company produced the small one to two inch Snow Babies. The Heber trademark consists of a shield with an "H" topped by a crown and the words "Made in Germany" underneath which is found scripted "Ges yesch." Karl Schneider created some of the more interesting action figures in the early 1900s. Some of those included Santa standing in a fireplace, Santa and a baby on a teeter-totter, and Santa riding a horse drawn coach. American mail-order houses soon began to carry such bisque figurines for sale. In 1910, when Marie Peary's brother was born,

Butler Brothers, 1923.

Sears and Roebuck sold sets of Snow Baby boys and girls, and Sears and Roebuck continued to sell these sets until 1923.

Most of these products disappeared from the market with the advent of World War II and others were packed away. One interesting point regarding identification of Snow Babies evolved from the start of World War II. Enterprising shopkeepers who did not want to pack away their offending German merchandise often removed "Germany" from the base. This has resulted in many collectors believing these to be older than those with stamps, because of the law which demanded that all items from exporting countries be marked with the country of origin after 1891. It must be further noted that some companies such as Karl Schneider used paper labels which through the years could have disappeared.

Collectors should be aware that Japan did manufacture similar bisque items in the 1930s and again in the 1950s. These are marked "Japan" and can be distinguished from their German counterparts since Japanese bisque figurines are most often poorly molded, unevenly painted, and very dull in color. German figures are carefully and exactly molded down to the ears of a teddy bear found in a sled pulled by Santa. Details such as eyes, brows, mouths, and other such features are fine and any paint added is bright in color. Bisque figurines continue to be made in Germany today, but they also lack the quality of earlier items. Single figurines are those most often reproduced, thus an ensemble of figures and action scenes will most likely be of the earlier vintage. Collectors need to check for distinguishing factors of the older figurines which include printed marks, mold numbers, and fine characteristics of the piece itself.

Chapter 9

GAMES, PUZZLES, AND TOYS

This particular category of Santa and Christmas items is highly collectible since the collecting of games, puzzles, and toys is an avid hobby of so many thousands of people. Toy collectors cross with Christmas collectors in vying for some very expensive items. However, novice collectors should not immediately forsake this area since numerous items, especially toys from the 1950s and 1960s, are relatively inexpensive at this time.

Christmas Games

With the Victorian fascination with parlor games, came the inevitable manufacturing of many Christmas and Santa related games to be played during the Christmas season. These were not manufactured in huge quantities since their use seemed only appropriate during a short period of the year. Parker Brothers produced, among countless other games, "The Card Game of Santa Claus," which is somewhat like Old Maid, except that the player holding the Santa card wins. In 1889, they manufactured "The Game of Merry Christmas," a board game. Each of these multi-colored puzzles or games would be a true delight since not many were manufactured and few have survived the ravages of time.

Christmas Puzzles

Wooden puzzles are of interest to collectors since the lithographed images of Father Christmas and later, Santa Claus, are some of the most beautiful. McLoughlin Brothers entered the game business too, and in 1889, turned its 1888 *Night Before Christmas* book into the "Santa Claus Cube Puzzle," using six of the book's color prints as block illustrations. In 1889, they also did an "Around the World with Santa Claus" and "Jolly Santa Picture Cubes." These are extremely rare due to the fact that very few of them are found today with each piece of the puzzle intact.

Christams Toys

Rare today are the pastile burners carved of wood in various figurals whose hollow bodies allowed the burning of pine incense. Also extremely rare are Noah's Arks, complete with animals, which held first spot in sales, followed by wooden rocking horses and colorfully painted wooden boats made in Thuringia. Some of the most famous soft plush animals were introduced by Margaret Steiff, originator of the Teddy Bear. Toys manufactured from iron, tin, and cardboard were often times Santa related.

Cast-Iron Toys

Among some of the finest old toys available are cast-iron toys made by Hubley, in the early 1900s. Cast-iron toys were manufactured by such companies as J. & E. Stevens of Cromwell, Connecticut; Ives, Blakeslee & Company of Bridgeport, Connecticut; and Pratt & Letchworth of Buffalo, New York. A fine example of such a toy is Father Christmas in a toy sleigh pulled by two reindeer. When the toy is pulled, the reindeer have a leaping action. The sleigh is decorated in white and gold with Father Christmas in red. Numerous still and mechanical cast-iron banks were produced from the late 1800s to the early 1900s. Still banks were excellently decorated with fine detail images of toys and trees. Mechanical banks were produced in abundance. In one particularly interesting bank Santa has a definition of snow on his gray clothing and hat. When the lever is pressed, he deposits the coin held in his raised right hand into the chimney.

Butler Brothers, 1923.

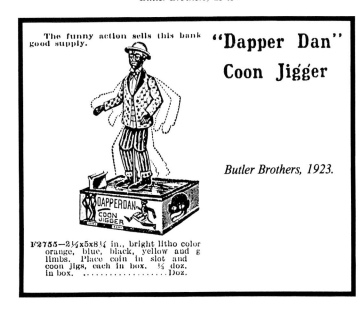

Butler Brothers, 1923.

Wind-up tin mechanical Santa, German. $1200-1400

Mechanical skating Santa, Japanese. $1000-1250

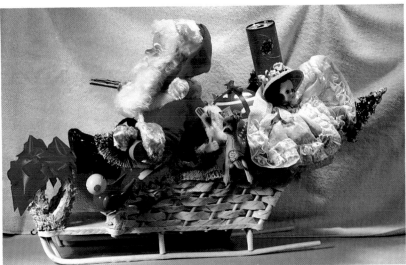

F.A.O. Schwarz sleigh with nodder reindeer, West Germany. $3000-3500

Elaborate wicker cart with toys including Toonerville Trolley Car, 1920s. $4000-4500

Wind-up and battery operated Japanese toys. Left, $160-175; Right, $185-200.

Plush snowman doll, 1960s. $90-100

Tin Toys

Toys of pressed tin were made in the Nuremberg area of Germany in the late 1700s. This area attracted the toymakers because of the workers' low wages and the number of skilled clockmakers who could also make parts for mechanical toys. The area had supplied wooden toys for many years, and the use of tinplate was a logical progression that could utilize existing marketing channels. Nodders and clockwork Santas were absolutely beautiful but, unfortunately very few of these managed to be saved. They were originally produced in 1855 by S. Guntermann. An extremely desirable toy window display item is the one in which Santa's head rocks back and forth and his eyes move from side to side set into motion by a metal clockworks behind this wood, cardboard, and paper item. Another fascinating item is the elaborate mechanical picture produced in the 1880s. It is made of wood and paper with a clockwork mechanism. In operation, Santa goes up and down peeking into the window. The boy beats the drum with his drumsticks as the girl cuddles her doll up and down. The boy in the center rocks back and forth on his rocking horse and grandfather bounces the baby on his knee. Paper lithography enabled the manufacturers to decorate even the most inexpensive toy with much color.

Tin toys began in the New England States during the 1830s. Such names as Francis, Ives, Brown, and Fallows were all spearheading the toy development in the United States. The toy industry in Europe was off to a slower start, but by 1850, manufacturers such as Marklin, Bing, and Lehmann began making an impact. Prior to 1850, there were several hundred toymakers in Nuremburg alone! By the turn of the century, the European toy industry was far superior to that of the United States. The duty on mechanical toys was levied according to weight, which meant that although American makers created some very fine cast toys, they would not have been commercially viable in the rest of the world. This tax on weight is one of the reasons why so may tinplate toys are so fragile, and rely on their decoration for much of their appeal. In 1903 there were less than one hundred American toy manufacturers and as late as 1914, over half of the toys in the United States were being imported from Europe. Especially desirable are the tin German toys such as those made after World War I, for Germany lost their dominance in this industry when the United States began mass producing toys. German-made toys such as Santa riding in mechanical cars, sleighs, and airplanes are highly collectible. Many of the Lehmann toys were mechanical, creating any number of effects through a wind-up mechanism. In these earliest days, toys were carefully hand-painted, individually assembled, and sometimes even hand-stenciled.

At the start of World War I, German-made toys were banned from the United States. This allowed the American manufacturer Louis Marx to exercise creativity in lithographed tin toys. Of all the American manufacturers, Ives is the best known, with its slogan "Ives toys make happy boys." As early as 1868, Edward Ives made movable dancing figures and an early Ives toy was a man who rowed his boat with two oars. In the 1930s and 1940s, the quality of toys declined greatly. In the years leading up to World War II, a large number of North Pole scenes, complete with tiny lead miniature figures of Santa, Mrs. Claus, the elves, reindeer, the Claus home, and his sleigh, were imported into this country. Coming mostly from Germany, they all were hand painted.

The 1950s were marked by the nearly total decline of German, French, English, and American-made toys with Japan becoming almost completely dominant. The tin mechanical toys manufactured in Japan from the 1930s through the 1950s are quickly being collected as history of this period. An exceptional piece is a battery operated walking Santa. In action he walks, beats the drum with his left arm, and rings the bell in his swinging right hand. He turns his head from side to side and the star-shaped light in his hat glows. He is made of metal and dressed in bright red and white cloth clothing. This Santa dates from the late 1940s.

Celluloid Toys

The Japanese manufactured a great number of celluloid toys in the 1950s. One of the more commonly found is a wind-up variety that has a moving sleigh, a leaping deer in the front, and a bell which rings in the back of the sleigh. The sleigh is of green metal with a white celluloid reindeer and a red and white celluloid Santa complete with toys and tree riding inside. In the 1960s, mechanicals including a tin Santa which turns the pages of a storybook and a Santa ringing a bell were produced. However, surprisingly few of these have survived even to today due to their breakability and the "throw away" generation that received these as Christmas presents.

Battery operated toy lanterns, 1950s and 1960s. $125-150 ea.

Opposite page: To Celluloid wind-up sleigh, Japanese, 1930s. $185-200 Bottom: Wind-up and battery opera Japanese toys, 19. and 1960s. Left, $180-195; Right, $140-180.

Chapter 10

CANDY MOLDS AND COOKIE CUTTERS

Imagine being a child in the early 1900s and looking into the store window of confectionery. Huge Father Christmas cookies and chocolate figures, teddy bears and a zoo of animals, as well as clowns and other human figures would dazzle and tempt your appetite. The vision of a candy store window is part of the charm behind the collecting of old molds and cookie cutters used to fashion these treats of years ago.

Molds and cookie cutters were often fashioned in the shape of Father Christmas. Some of the earliest of molds were created by the gingerbread bakers and lebkuchen creators, who were also chandlers (or wax workers). After about the mid-1600s, molds were made from carved wood or molded plaster. Earlier, molds were of fired, unglazed clay. Until only recently, glazed clay molds were used to make marzipan. Most of those molds found are from the late 1800s into the early 20th century and were made of carved pear wood. Needing a more durable and easier to use mold, metal was turned to.

Candy Molds

Chocolate molds date back to the 1880s. As early as 1876, the Swiss were molding chocolate into solid bars. Reaching their zenith of popularity in the 1920s, these European made molds all but disappeared. Most molds were made in Germany, France, and England. Reiche, Dresden made molds of outstanding quality often with fluted edgings. Eppelsheimer & Company were the principal American manufacturers of both chocolate and ice cream molds. Metal molds were easy to produce in large numbers, plus they were more durable. Candy molds used to make hard candy in the shape of Santa Claus were made of heavy metal and had surprisingly good detail. Extra large molds, up to twenty-four inches high, were made for special occasions. They were rented out by the mold manufacturer to the chocolate shops who put Father Christmas figures in the window to attract buyers. It took ten pounds of chocolate to make a hollow figure in the mold. Chocolate molds are held together by round clips or clothes-pin-like clamps about an inch and a half long. These were used principally for the German mold with fluted edgings which allowed for greater contouring. Other molds have hinges which were added by the chocolate makers to eliminate clipping one side and therefore speeding up production. Besides two-piece molds there are one-sided molds in forms ranging from mice to Father Christmas.

In addition, flat one-piece trays, either multi-figured or with repeated figures, were also manufactured. The rarest of chocolate and candy molds include those three and four piece molds. Any numbers found on molds themselves are the stock numbers. If there is a large single number, it indicates that these molds were made in a series and only those with matching numbers fit together exactly. If the mold is marked "Holland Handicrafts" it would indicate a mold no older than 15 years, even though it is made in the original antique casts and is identical to the old molds. In recent years, even this identification has been eliminated so new molds are identifiable by their excellent condition and the model. Even ice cream and cake molds in various Santa shapes have been found.

Cookie Cutters

Cookie cutters come to the fore at any holiday but at none more than the Christmas season. Thousands of traditional Santas, fir trees, bells, stars, and gingerbread men have been delighting children for decades.

The very first cookies, as we know them today, probably appeared at the start of the industrial age when the cook stove supplanted the fireplace and Dutch oven for cooking and baking. Housewives soon discovered that dough baked in the form of cookies had advantages over the cake in large pans.

When inexpensive tin sheets began to be produced in the 1850s, cookie cutters made their debut. Tin-plated sheet metal was cut and readily shaped with a hammer. Any fastening was done with solder. Tin, being the chief ingredient of solder, fused nicely to insure a solid joint. The earliest of cookie cutters were fashioned in many home workshops and were round in shapes without a handle. The tinware market was dominant in Pennsylvania and Connecticut, especially Berlin where the local tinsmiths were real craftsmen. Many of the early hand-made cookie cutters had a solid tin backing attached to the bent design with its cutting edge. Soldered to the backing was a handle under which one, or perhaps two, holes were punched to allow air to ease the cookie out of its form. These early solid-back cookie cutters are not easy to find and they continue to rise steeply in price. But they are in surprisingly good condition considering they are formed from malleable tin. The shapes are various; some are round, heart, or star-shaped. But most, it seems, are figures of Santa, animals, birds, or children. Animal forms include a rabbit, pig, rooster, horse, dog, turkey, and chick.

Twentieth century cookie cutters, tin, aluminum, or plastic, are made in so many shapes that it defies classification. Some cutters have nooth edges while others are more decorative with fluted or scalloped orders. In the 1930s, during the transition from auction to contract ridge, cutters in the forms of spade, heart, diamond, and club became opular for bridge parties and for use at Christmas. Even the cutters om the 1940s and 1950s are quite interesting as many of them had uite defined shapes. A modern adaptation of a single cookie cutter is a roup of assorted designs concentrated in one gadget. The cutters may e mounted on a wheel to roll over the dough or they may be arranged o move quickly by hand from one shape to another.

Few early cookie cutters were marked with identification. Some ree-shaped cutters from the 1930s are found with the marking "G.M.T 'o. Czechoslovakia." It is possible for collectors to specialize in a paricular form or a particular era; furthermore, even the possibility of ollecting cutters issued by baking companies to advertise their prodcts. Many of these molds and cutters can make an interesting wall isplay during the Christmas season. Regardless, collectors should conult more specialized books on this topic if interested in cookie cutters.

Butler Brothers, 1905.

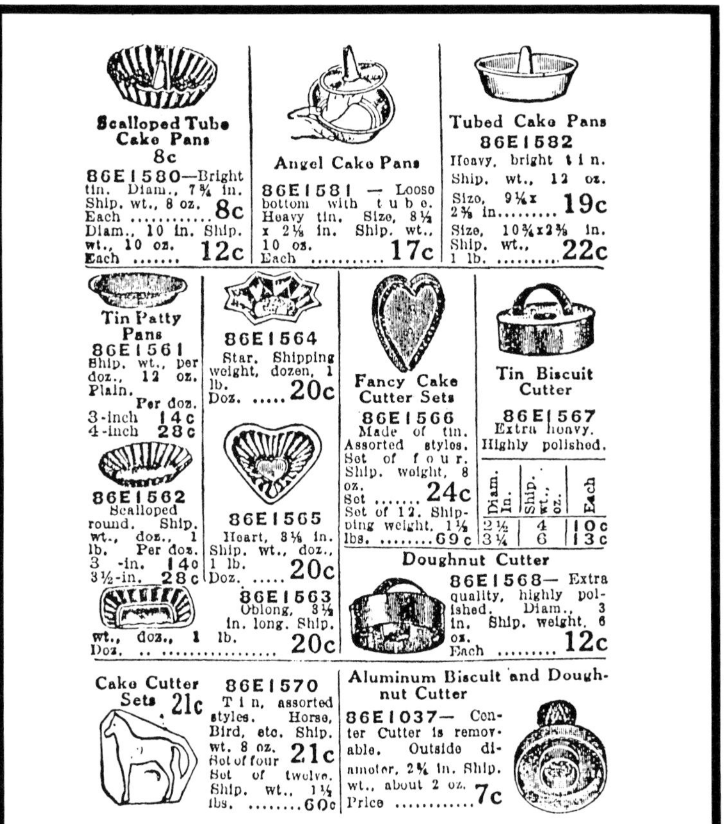
Scalloped Tube Cake Pans 8c
86E1580—Bright tin. Diam., 7¾ in. Ship. wt., 8 oz. Each 8c
Diam., 10 in. Ship. wt., 10 oz. Each 12c

Angel Cake Pans
86E1581 — Loose bottom with tube. Heavy tin. Size, 8¼ x 2⅛ in. Ship. wt., 10 oz. Each 17c

Tubed Cake Pans
86E1582
Heavy, bright tin. Ship. wt., 12 oz.
Size, 9¼x 2⅜ in......... 19c
Size, 10¾x2⅜ in. Ship. wt., 1 lb. 22c

Tin Patty Pans
86E1561
Ship. wt., per doz., 12 oz. Plain. Per doz.
3-inch 14c
4-inch 28c

86E1562
Scalloped round. Ship. wt., doz., 1 lb. Per doz.
3 -in. 14c
3½-in. 28c

86E1564
Star. Shipping weight, dozen, 1 lb. Doz. 20c

86E1565
Heart, 3⅛ in. Ship. wt., doz., 1 lb. Doz. 20c

86E1563
Oblong, 3½ in. long. Ship. wt., doz., 1 lb. Doz. 20c

Fancy Cake Cutter Sets
86E1566
Made of tin. Assorted styles. Set of four. Ship. weight, 8 oz. Set 24c
Set of 12. Shipping weight, 1¼ lbs. 69c

Tin Biscuit Cutter
86E1567
Extra heavy. Highly polished.

Diam. in.	Ship. wt., oz.	Each
2¼	4	10c
3¼	6	13c

Doughnut Cutter
86E1568— Extra quality, highly polished. Diam., 3 in. Ship. weight, 6 oz. Each 12c

Cake Cutter Sets 21c
86E1570
Tin, assorted styles. Horse, Bird, etc. Ship. wt. 8 oz. Set of four 21c
Set of twelve. Ship. wt., 1½ lbs. 60c

Aluminum Biscuit and Doughnut Cutter
86E1037— Center Cutter is removable. Outside diameter, 2¾ in. Ship. wt., about 2 oz. Price 7c

Butler Brothers, 1925.

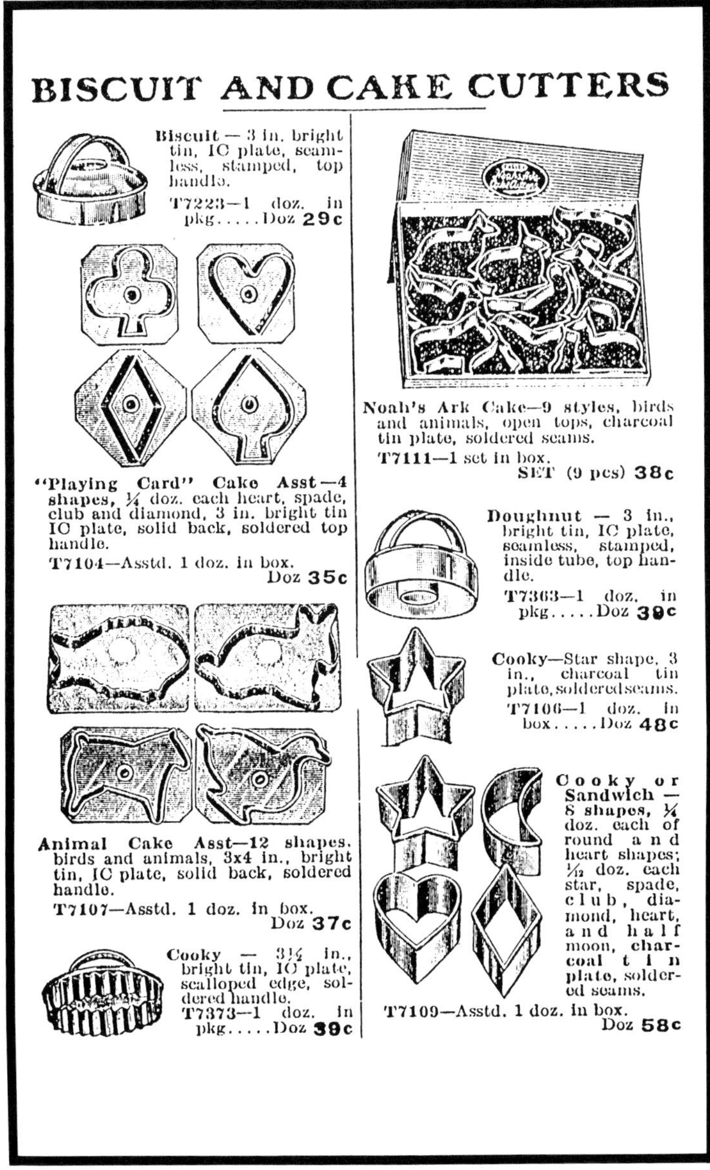
BISCUIT AND CAKE CUTTERS

Biscuit — 3 in. bright tin, IC plate, seamless, stamped, top handle.
T7223—1 doz. in pkg.....Doz 29c

"Playing Card" Cake Asst—4 shapes, ¼ doz. each heart, spade, club and diamond, 3 in. bright tin IC plate, solid back, soldered top handle.
T7104—Asstd. 1 doz. in box. Doz 35c

Animal Cake Asst—12 shapes, birds and animals, 3x4 in., bright tin, IC plate, solid back, soldered handle.
T7107—Asstd. 1 doz. in box. Doz 37c

Cooky — 3¼ in., bright tin, IC plate, scalloped edge, soldered handle.
T7373—1 doz. in pkg.....Doz 39c

Noah's Ark Cake—9 styles, birds and animals, open tops, charcoal tin plate, soldered seams.
T7111—1 set in box. SET (9 pcs) 38c

Doughnut — 3 in., bright tin, IC plate, seamless, stamped, inside tube, top handle.
T7363—1 doz. in pkg.....Doz 39c

Cooky—Star shape, 3 in., charcoal tin plate, soldered seams.
T7106—1 doz. in box.....Doz 48c

Cooky or Sandwich — 8 shapes, ¼ doz. each of round and heart shapes; ½ doz. each star, spade, club, diamond, heart, and half moon, charcoal tin plate, soldered seams.
T7109—Asstd. 1 doz. in box. Doz 58c

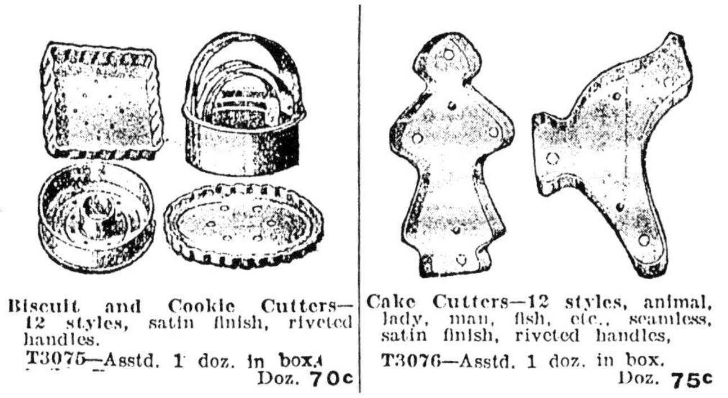
Biscuit and Cookie Cutters—12 styles, satin finish, riveted handles.
T3075—Asstd. 1 doz. in box. Doz. 70c

Cake Cutters—12 styles, animal, lady, man, fish, etc., seamless, satin finish, riveted handles.
T3076—Asstd. 1 doz. in box. Doz. 75c

Butler Brothers, 1923.

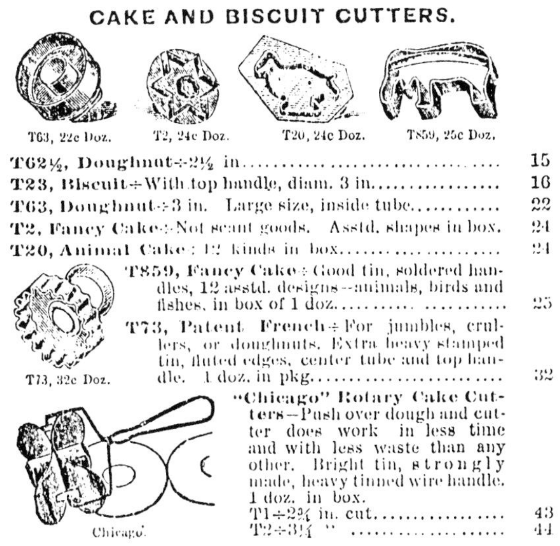
CAKE AND BISCUIT CUTTERS.

T63, 22c Doz. T2, 24c Doz. T20, 24c Doz. T859, 25c Doz.

T62½, Doughnut÷2½ in.	15
T23, Biscuit÷With top handle, diam. 3 in.	16
T63, Doughnut÷3 in. Large size, inside tube	22
T2, Fancy Cake÷Not seam goods. Asstd. shapes in box.	24
T20, Animal Cake: 12 kinds in box	24
T859, Fancy Cake÷Good tin, soldered handles, 12 asstd. designs—animals, birds and fishes, in box of 1 doz.	25
T73, Patent French÷For jumbles, crullers, or doughnuts. Extra heavy stamped tin, fluted edges, center tube and top handle. 1 doz. in pkg.	32

T73, 32c Doz.

"Chicago" Rotary Cake Cutters—Push over dough and cutter does work in less time and with less waste than any other. Bright tin, strongly made, heavy tinned wire handle. 1 doz. in box.

T1÷2¾ in. cut	43
T2÷3¼ "	44

Chicago.

Chapter 11

ELECTRIC LIGHTS SOME INTERESTING VARIATIONS

The figural light bulb has become quite collectible in recent years with European clear painted glass and the Japanese milk glass variety being the most publicized. However, there are other types of collectible bulbs that are even more rare and gaining more respect from Christmas collectors since these too are becoming more difficult to find with each passing year.

Celluloid Lights

Celluloid lamps are among the rarest of electric light collectibles. These experimental lights were basically an outgrowth of the celluloid children's toys which were popular at the time. "Celluloid" lights, from the late teens, operated on a parallel-wired cord, but were around 3 volts and used a transformer or dry cells as the power source. Produced with eight to ten lamps per set, these were actually small lamps mounted inside thin figurals, made in Japan, formed of an early plastic called celluloid. These early sets came with a wooden base switch. Celluloid was extremely flammable and care had to be taken in its use, thus one reason for their lower voltage and lower heat. The detail and color was very well done from tiny 3/4" fish up to 6" cherubs.

There were such figures as fish, horses, dogs, fruits, and birds. In the mid to late 1920s, NOMA sold once again a series of Japanese produced celluloid lamp covers in traditional Christmas figures as done in the late teens. Because of the fire hazard, these were manufactured for only a short period and should not be confused with the Fancy Figures, a colorful plastic lamp cover introduced by NOMA in 1952. There were primarily Santas, angels, snowmen, and birds with very few animals being produced, for C-6 and C-7 lamp sets. They also did not hold up well due to the heat of the lamps, and frequently cracked or were broken after a short time.

Rare celluloid lights. $240-300 ea.

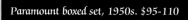
Paramount boxed set, 1950s. $95-110

Paramount bubble lights, late 1950s. $125-135

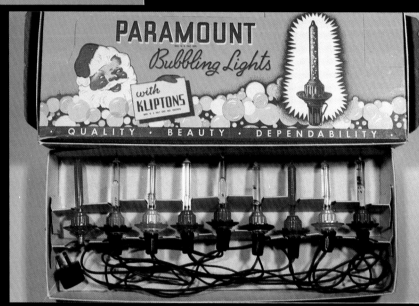

Noma boxed set, 1950s. $90-100

Noma bubble lights, late 1950s. $90-100

Bubble Lights

"Watch them Bubble," glamour Light your Christmas Tree with Paramount Bubbling Lights, and "Watch them rise, watch them fall." These are only a few of the slogans used to help sell these phenomenons of the mid-1940s and 1950s: BUBBLE LIGHTS. For a brief period of history, there was hardly a home that did not have at least one string of these lights on its Christmas tree. Perhaps much of their charm lay in the action of the bubbles, for not since the use of candles was there some motion on the decorated tree.

It is this mystery of motion that causes many admirers to question the components of bubble lights. The basic elements of the bubble light are a light bulb, a tube of a special liquid, and a plastic base to house both items. Most bubble lights were made in the C-6 miniature base format, though many were made in the C-7 candelabra base and recently also made in the midget variety, with both push-in and screw-in bases. The bulbs in most are flat-topped which allows the liquid to rest on top, thus gathering as much heat as possible from the lamp. In nearly all cases, the base is two halves of plastic either glued together or held together by interlocking teeth (as in the case of a Paramount brand). The bases were of colored plastic—red, green, blue, yellow, orange, pink, white, purple, and several variations on the shades of each color.

The tube of liquid is what sets the bubble light into its own unique category. The liquid is a special low-boiling chemical sealed in a glass vial which has had the air evacuated allowing the liquid to boil from the heat of the bulb, then condense once the bubbles have reached to the top of the liquid. This process is explicitly described in the patent filed June 9, 1945, by A. Abramson. "The liquid is of low boiling and I may employ fluids such as, for example, wood alcohol, ether, or methylene chloride. If it is desired to enhance the ornamental effect, the liquid, tube, or both may be colored or a thin film of pellucid coloring matter coated on the inner or outer surfaces of the tube. Only a portion of the tube is filled in liquid, the balance of the tube being evacuated so as to provide a partial vacuum in which vapor (bubbles) generated in the lower end of the tube may condense and return to the body of the liquid."

The liquid, methylene chloride, is a low boiling, flammable, poisonous fluid. This liquid inside has an extremely strong chemical odor and dries instantaneously, permanently staining anything it has touched, so collectors should be careful if a tube were to break. The white granules, either separated or in large clumps, found in the bottom of the tube are the "bubble generators," and are usually, but not limited to, sugar, borax, and table salt. Another item found in many bubble light tubes is a glass pellet seated near the bottom of the tube. This pellet "catches" the tiny bubbles, "gathering" them up before they are forced between the pellet and glass tube, up into the liquid column. This produces the large bubbles that rise up in the liquid. Those bubble lights without the gas pellets in the vials produce very tiny bubbles.

The beginning of the bubble light idea began with Carl Otis. He filed a patent on November 27, 1935, for Bubbling Display Signs. These signs were designed to spell out a word or to identify a symbol. The glass tube letters or designs were hollow, filled with methylene chloride or a similar compound, properly exhausted, and when heat was applied to the base of the display unit holding the glass tubes, they produced a bubbling effect. Christmas tree bubbling lights were not mentioned in this particular patent. Up until a few years ago, it was believed NOMA did not market the Bubble light until 1946. However, through some ads and patent information, the year can now be established as 1945 or earlier since boxed sets have been located which indicate a patent #2,174,445, granted September 29, 1939. It would seem most unusual that a product granted a patent in 1939 would not be put onto the market until 1945, since the granted date was two years before the United States entered the war. In situations where products were being put into production waiting on a patent to be granted, it is simply marked "Patent Applied For." Then that information is substituted for the actual patent number once it has been obtained.

NOMA Electric of New York was the only company of the ten that Otis approached which was willing to take a gamble on this new idea, and gave Otis a royalty of three cents per lamp sold. Other companies were quick to pick up on the idea and soon marketed their own versions of the bubbler. Most notable of these companies was Raylite Electric of New York. John Petry, an assignor to Raylite, filed his patent on May 6, 1946, and was granted a patent on December 3, 1946. He claimed improved devices, liquids and improved construction of the bubbling light. At first they were called Paramount "Kristal Snow Animated Candle Lights." They were "oil" filled, the liquid being made of two types: (1) an organic oil such as rape seed, castor, or cod liver oils, and (2) methylene chloride, chloroform, or ether. When mixed they produced a slower flow of bubbles, much smaller in size and in greater quantities, without the glass pellet in the tube. The name "Bubble Lite" was not used, specifically to avoid patent infringement on the Bubble Lite Trade Mark.

NOMA filed suit against the competition, but was offered a settlement out of court, giving Otis a similar royalty offer to the one he was getting from NOMA. However, Otis refused the offer, the case went on to court and was lost. Otis lost all royalties and no doubt was upset more than once after that, because the bubble light soon came to be the hottest item on the market, lasting for a period of at least two decades. Thus, the market was opened for a huge burst of bubble lights by other companies. In all, approximately thirty plus different styles and brands of bubble lights were manufactured. The word "Lite" was used by NOMA, Glo-Lite (a "generic" brand of NOMA), Reliance, and Renown. "Light" was used by Paramount, Sterling (a "generic" brand of Paramount), Holly, and Grant. Of the many styles, NOMA and Paramount are the most common, with Polly, Peerless Shooting Star, Yule Glow, Amico, C-7 Rocket Ships, the C-7 oil Paramounts, and the C-7 Shooting Stars being the most difficult to find.

A most unusual bubble light is the Peerless Shooting Star. They have a small amount of heavier liquid that does not mix with the regular liquid. The bubbles are formed in this thick liquid, then spring up into the thin liquid, but because of their weight, cascade back down, similar to a 4th of July fireworks fountain or a juggling effect. The way to distinguish an unlighted Shooting Star is to turn it upside down and study the fluid in the tube. If it separates into two obvious types, the larger section being the lighter fluid, you probably have a Shooting Star.

A related collectible in this area is the bubble light tree made in a variety of sizes. The smallest is an 8-light tree and the largest, over three feet tall with 20 lights. Sockets were wired into the branches so that lights can be replaced as they burn out. These trees came in green or white and both C-6 and C-7 candelabra size bases. Another style of tree, quite rare, is similar to the bubble light tree. However, it has one standard base lamp in the hollow center which heats tubes of liquid which extend out of the branches. Also there were plastic snowmen

...can

...con-

...do.

...vari-

...Cre-

...the

...de of

...low-

and

...bble.

...An-

...may

...ough

...When

...used

...much

...tage/

...e the

...n the

...es of

...place

...diffi-

Middle: C-7 Rocket ship bubble light.

Left: "Kristal Snow Animated Candle Light," 1946.

Right: Peerless shooting star.

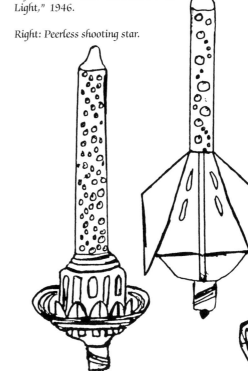

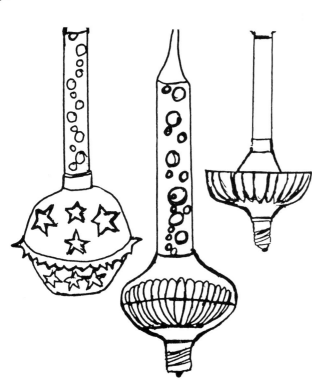

Left: "Clip on" bubble light.

Middle: Noma bubble light, 1950s.

Right: "Matchless" bubble light, late 1930s.

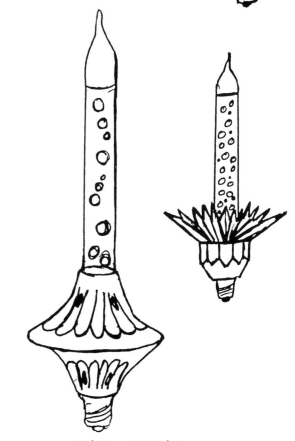

Left: Noma's 1948 design.

Right: "Reliance Spark-L-Lite".

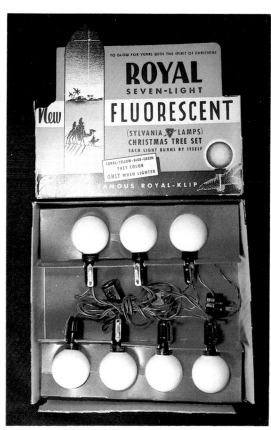

Whirl-Glo Shades-boxed set, 1930s. $85-95

Boxed set of fluorescent lights, 1950s. $130-150

Opposite page:
Top: Plastic cased and assorted
lights. $50-75 ea.
Bottom: Electric light
variations. $100-140 ea.

"Dresden" cased bulbs, late 1920s. $250-275 ea.

Fluorescent Lights

Another relatively recent, but very interesting electric light, is the fluorescent lamp sets which were introduced in 1945; they lasted less than two years. Unlit, they appear to be plain white balls with a black skirted base. But when lit, they come alive in soft glowing colors of yellow, green, blue, coral (red), and orchid (purple); the colors being marked on the base. They are 120 volt, C-7 base. They were sold in sets of seven bulbs by Sylvania, Royal and Miller companies; replacement bulbs were sold in boxes of ten. They have no filament but work on the same principle as the long tube fluorescent bulbs in kitchen and office fixtures. The white coating is just plain white paint as in some ordinary household lamps. The color exhibited is due to the color of the gaseous element inside the bulb. Each gas element known to science glows with a specific color when ionized. Argon created the blue and green bulbs; neon created the coral, yellow, and orchid bulbs. The inside of the bulb is coated with colored phosphors. The type of gas used inside was matched as closely as possible to the color of the phosphors in the white coating. (The green is bright because green phosphor is the brightest member of the chemical family and red phosphor is the dimmest. A standard 4-foot fluorescent tube in green is three to five times brighter than a red one of the same size.) The ions created by the glowing gas bombard the phosphor coating causing it to fluoresce, or glow. This is the definition of a fluorescent light source. The hue can be varied somewhat by changing the pressure and/or varying the current at the electrodes, and gases can be alloyed in various proportions to provide color combinations not available with single gases. The prices of these when new were very expensive compared to a regular set of tungsten lamps and even the individual lamps were around fifty cents to one dollar compared to ten cents or two for fifteen cents for milk glass tungsten bulbs.

"Dresden" and Plastic Cased Lights

NOMA's "Dresden" lights made in 1928 were very large glass figural shells imported from Germany in beautifully painted shapes of animals, flowers, Santas, and so forth. In 1927, a patent was issued in behalf of Bernhardt Haupt's invention of a double electric socket that would hold a replaceable light bulb on one end. This was inserted into the bottom of a hollow glass figure, and then threaded end screwed into the socket of a light bulb string. Each light covered a plain C-6 lamp housed in a brass adaptor fitting. The brass housing then screwed into a brass collar in the figural—the idea being that burned out lamps could be replaced for continued enjoyment of the lighted figural. One of the most novel is a special six inch body of Santa holding a Christmas tree. The paint did not hold up very well, and it is difficult to find one that is not flaking. To prevent this, a collector can coat the figure with a clear varnish or with colorless nail polish in places where the paint is chipping. Unfortunately, the brass housing easily corroded and stuck to the collar so burned out lamps could not be replaced. (With much patience, a needle or similar thin tool, and a solvent material such as WD-40, these brass fittings can eventually be loosened and the Dresden once again enjoyed.)

In spite of their luminous beauty on the tree, the drawback to these figures was the fact that their size and weight made them a bit awkward to be used successfully on Christmas trees. However, these were advertised as lights to be used year around, on birthdays, Halloween, and other such occasions. It was this versatility that kept them on the market for a number of years.

In 1952, the bulb-case idea was used by NOMA with their "Fancy Figures" which were C-6 and C-7 lamps covered by a plastic figure of a Santa, snowman, angel, or animal. Each had a hole in the bottom for a replaceable light bulb. The flame resistant figure was usually red or white, and the angel had a nice clear plastic halo which reflected the light from inside. Unfortunately, the heat from the lamp frequently melted and disfigured the cover. These were also available in a snap-on variety which snapped over a plain C-7 lamp.

Noma catalog, 1954.

The Japanese also produced bulb-cased sets of lights during the 1930s. Small cardboard houses with a built-in lamp in the roof were made in at least a dozen different styles with cellophane windows for the light to show through. They were marked "Nippon Registration #71616" on the bottom of the base.

Shaded Lights

When sales of novelty lights began to lag in the mid-1930s, the idea of motion for the tree was offered to tempt Christmas light purchasers. "Whirl-Glo Shades," made by the Sail-Me Company in Chicago, 1936, were delightful accent items made of treated paper and formed into cone shapes with special folds at the top. A paper "cap" with a sharp pin was placed on a plain C-6 lamp and the shade then set on the pin. The heat from the lamp would cause the shade to revolve. The shades had pictures printed in brilliant colorful detail. The time and effort taken in adjusting the shades for perfect balance was well rewarded by their action and delightful variety. They were sold five or ten to a boxed set with religious and secular designs available. Instructions on the boxes suggested that the cones be glued to the bulbs to make them more stable. This resulted in their loss after the bulbs burned out, and explains to collectors today why so many sets are found missing the cones. Generally sold for ten and twenty-five cents a box, a few were sold for five cents. All of the cones and shades were treated to make them flame-proof.

Later in the 1930s, Sunbeam Specialty Company of Cleveland, Ohio, solved the problem of balancing the cone on the bulb by introducing, in its place, a spring-shaped piece of wire with a pointed tip to balance the shade. The top of the shade was redesigned to contain a flat disk of metal with slits and a tiny, upside-down glass cup to balance on the pin instead of the indented metal bar used in the Whirl-Glo shades. Made of waxed paper, they were sold only as a set of eight with scenes depicting various Christmas activities. Since they are a product of the Depression years, many were giveaways and could be sent for with a coupon packed with other paper products.

Perhaps the most successful was a set of Walt Disney plastic shades decorated with Disney characters. NOMA's "Mickey Mouse Shades," actually made in 1935, were introduced at the 1939 New York World's Fair. These were bell shaped plastic shades in various colors which covered a plain C-6 lamp. The shades were decorated with decals of Mickey Mouse and friends by special permission for Walt Disney. Other similar sets featured Mother Goose, Popeye, Katzenjammer, and Silly Symphony and were nice accessory items for C-6 lamps.

In the late 1950s, the Tinkle Toy Company of Youngstown, Ohio, updated the revolving paper shade by forming shades of plastic, with a small aluminum pinwheel balanced on a pin inside. These shades are remembered by many Americans since they were extremely popular at that time. These were intended to be hung over or near the bulbs, not actually on them, because by this date, the majority of electric lights used 120 volts instead of 15 and generated a great deal of heat. The new shades looked more like bird cages, and finding one without the original box to identify its use could easily confuse the younger Christmas collector.

Twinkle and Miniature Lights

When collectors think of "twinkle" lights, they think of a relatively recent innovation, but they have been in existence for a number of years and early boxed sets are almost impossible to locate. Some "twinkle" lights were made for C-6 sets in the 1930s, but they caused the whole sets to go on and off and were not popular. Interestingly enough, these twinkle lights were sometimes made in clear glass figural shapes such as an embossed star on a round disk, a rose, a pine

Noma catalog, 1954.

cone, and a full figure elf, identified by an extra large base collar. These lamps had a built-in flashing mechanism made from a bimetallic strip. When electricity passed through this strip toward the filament, like a thermostat, it would get warm and bend slightly, breaking the electrical flow, and the light would go out. As it cooled, it would bend back and reconnect the flow.

Several different companies in the late 1950s produced special sets of twinkle lights operating on transformers. The lamps (either cone or tube shaped) were C-6 miniature based, 6-8 volt, used on a special cord, wired in multiple, and connected to a transformer. The transformer, though, was too heavy and impractical for extensive decorating.

Twinkle lights gained popularity in the 1950s for use on C-7 and C-9 sets. These cone-shaped lamps, painted in bright transparent colors, were pleasing when mixed with steady burning lamps, especially in outdoor decorating.

A most unusual C-7 twinkle lamp (its name currently unknown) was produced by the Paramount Company probably in the 1950s. It had a black plastic base similar to the Sylvania Fluorescents, and, and the white glass appeared much the same except tube shaped. Inside were actually two narrow tube-shaped twinkle lamps each painted in two or three transparent colors. When lit, the outside white surface glowed a mixture of five or six colors; and these colors changed as the two twinkle lamps inside began to blink independently.

The rising technology of the 1950s created a desire for something new, and out of Italy came the "midget" lights—tiny 1/2" bright lights—and not the usual eight on a string but up to 35, 50, or even 100. They were equipped with shunt devices so if one burned out, the others would remain lit. And most of them were designed in straight line construction. They had a "space age" appearance and swept the country in the 1960s, forcing the C-6 to nearly disappear from the market entirely. (One last revival attempt at marketing C-6 was sponsored by NOMA around 1981 with some success.)

The first midget lamps were wired directly onto the cord. Replacing a burned out lamp was sometimes impossible. Later, American and Japanese sets used lamps with tiny screw bases. Then along came the current "push-in" lamps. The lamp is housed in a plastic base with the two lamp wires folded back against each side of the base. The base is then pushed into a socket where the wires make contact with the base connection.

However, the lamps are still wired in standard series basis and sets are not foolproof. The wires are thin and break easily, and it's more frustrating going through 35 or 50 lamps to find the problem instead of the old-fashioned eight. Consequently, thousands of these sets are trashed each year by consumers who don't have the time, patience, or knowledge to check for the problem. Midget lights are currently popular due to their light weight, versatility, and low price. Many now are being made weatherproof for outdoor use.

Americans continued to search for "new" ideas and promoted sets with plastic covers of people, animals, fruits, etc., OVER the midget lamps. With a few obvious differences of material and quality, it seems we're back to the same idea of figural light bulbs of thirty to seventy years ago! And a recent variety from the 1980s had plastic covers in the same shape, only smaller, of the common C-6 fluted lamp.

GE's midget lamp line, "Merry Midget," included plastic covers of Santas, post lamps, kerosene and tinsel sprays. But their most unusual midget lamp product was the "Twinklettes." Twenty light sets consisted of ten regular midget lamps and ten specially constructed twinkle lamps which blinked on and off but left the regular lights burning constantly, giving a pleasant variety to midget twinkle lamp sets.

Japanese milk glass bulbs, 1930s and 1940s. $80-200 ea.

Japanese milk glass bulbs, 1930s. $100-200 ea.

Opposite page: *Rare early festoon lights on left and clear European figurals on right. $160-250 ea.*

Statue of Liberty bulb, extremely rare. $1200-1300

Milk glass figurals from Japan. $40-120 ea.

CHRISTMAS TREE CANDLE HOLDERS.

F1085, 57c Gro.   F3654, and F3655.   F1086, 69c Gro.   F3656, 36c Doz.   F3657, 37c Doz.

F1085—Ball candle holder. Wire about 5 in., heavy ball Gro. weight, wire hanger. Asstd. red, blue and gold. ½ gro. in box..$0 57

F3654—1½ in., tin, in colors, shell design, four prongs, strong clip and spring. ½ doz. on card, 1 gro. in box..   59

F1086—Elastic or extension, 5¼ in., malleable tin, asstd. colors, can be adjusted to any angle. For either Christmas tree or birthday cakes. 1 gro. in box..............   69

F3655—2 in. leaf saucer, fancy colors, strong spring clip. ½ doz. on card. 1 gro. in box........................   75

F3656—1¼ in. colored isinglass cup, candle and spring Doz. bottom holder, serves as an ornament as well as holder. 1 doz. in box..$0 36

F3657—Asstd. matt finish blown glass globe, 3 in., floral design, variegated tints, metal spring, 4 prong holder. 1 doz. in box..   37

F3658—Floral design blown glass globe, asstd. tints on patent ball bearing spring holder, 3¾ in. ½ doz. in box..........................   72

F3659—1¾ in. blown glass globe, colored stripes, metal air wheel at top, spring attachment, upright wire rod, globe revolves when candle burns. ½ doz. in box.....................   75

F3658, 72c Doz.   F3659, 75c Doz.

Butler Brothers, 1905.

Montgomery Wards, mid-1930s.

CHRISTMAS TREE AND DECORATIVE ELECTRIC LIGHT OUTFITS.

Extremely popular for store window display and home use. Furnished without batteries. Each outfit in box.

4F1843, Multiple Battery Outfit — Consists of 17 ft. wire, two 6 ft. strands with 5 ft. leader, junction box, 8 sockets, clear and asstd. color lamps, box for 3 batteries.
Outfit, **$1.75**

4F1844, Electric Light Outfit — About 35 ft. wire, pendant sockets 18 clear and asstd. color lamps, large connecting plug.
Outfit, **$4.00**

4F1845—As 4F1844, 24 lights, junction box and extra wire....................Outfit, **$6.00**

Electric Lights for 4F1843 Tree Outfit.
4F1805—Plain............Doz. $1.44
4F1806—Red.......... " 1.50
4F1807—Blue............ " 1.50

Lamps for 4F1844 and 4F1845 Outfits.
4F1808—Plain............Doz. $1.48
4F1809—Red .... " 1.56
4F1810—Blue. .... " 1.56
4F1811—Green .... " 1.56

Butler Brothers, 1911.

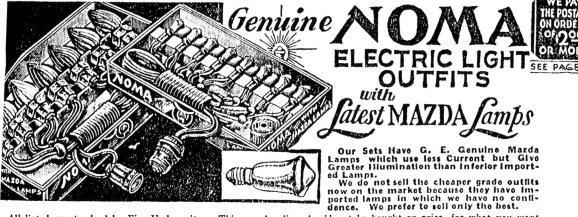

Genuine NOMA ELECTRIC LIGHT OUTFITS *with* Latest MAZDA Lamps

WE PAY THE POSTAGE ON ORDERS OF $2.00 OR MORE
SEE PAGE 2

Our Sets Have G. E. Genuine Mazda Lamps which use less Current but Give Greater Illumination than Inferior Imported Lamps.

We do not sell the cheaper grade outfits now on the market because they have imported lamps in which we have no confidence. We prefer to sell only the best.

All listed as standard by Fire Underwriters. This merchandise should not be bought on price, for what you want is lasting qualities. This can only be had by purchasing Noma Outfits. No Transformer necessary. Have patented Tachon connector for extra strings on house currents up to 120 volts. Not to be used on battery or on 32-volt lighting outfit current. Do not confuse Mazda lamp sets with cheap carbon or imported lamp sets which can be sold for much lower prices, but cannot be depended upon. Our outfits are furnished with assorted colored lamps.

Weatherproof Outdoor Set with Chipproof Inside Coloring Lamps

If one lamp goes out, the rest remain lit. Has extension connector to add more strings of lights and sliding wood beads to help fasten sockets to branches. Seven 120-volt genuine C9¼ inside coloring Mazda lamps connected in multiple, making each light burn independently of the others. Do not confuse with lower priced sets having outside coloring lamps which chip.

49F6594—7 Light Outfit Bakelite sockets.**$2.79**
Postpaid

49F6595—Box of 2 inside colored lamps. Shpg. wt., ¾ lb................................37c

Famous New Mazda Bell Lamp Eight-Light Series Sets

Attention! These sets have new perfected G. E. Bell Shaped Mazda lamps, series wired, knotted with sliding red enameled wood beads, enabling you to fasten sockets to branch in a secure, upright position. Extension connector to add more strings.

49F6571—Complete outfit, 8 lights. **$1.49**
Shpg. wt., 2 lbs.

49F6572—Complete outfit, 16 lights.
Postpaid....................................**$2.93**

49F6573—Complete outfit, 24 lights.
Postpaid.......................................4.29

49F6575—Box of 3 assorted colored bell shaped new type G. E. Mazda Lamps. Shpg. wt., ¾ lb....29c

Loop Circuit Genuine Mazda Set to Meet the Demand for Lower Priced Sets

Do not confuse with cheaper imported lamp sets. Eight flame shape Mazda lamps in composition sockets. **89c**
49F6570—8-Light set with plug and connector. Shpg. wt., 1½ lbs.........................
49F6588—3 flame shape Mazda bulbs for above outfit. Shpg. wt., 6 oz........................25c

111

Chapter 12

NEW DISCOVERIES IN CHRISTMAS LIGHTS AND ORNAMENTS

Numerous collectors across this country have given permission for many new never-before-seen ornaments to be photographed for this book. Contained in the following pages is an array of new ornaments not previously recorded. Each of these is arranged in the categories used in the price guide of *Christmas Past* so that the same format will allow Christmas enthusiasts to easily locate and re-locate these decorations.

Opposite page:

Top left: Lithographed horse and child clip-ons. Left, $300-325; Right, $120-150.

Top right: Lithographed bird tin clip-ons. Left, $145-160; Right, $120-140.

Bottom left: Heavily embossed tin clip-ons. Left, $250-300; Right, $100-120.

Bottom right: Child tin clip-on. $300-325

Flashed tin bird clip-on. $250-300

Lithographed Santa clip-on. $300-325

Lantern candleholder with glass windows, from France. $225-260

Hanging lantern with glass shades. $110-130

Heavy glass candle lantern. $90-110

Paper candle lantern, early 1900s. $120-140

Hanging tin candle lantern with gelatin windows. $145-160

Quilted glass oil lantern. $60-75

Two sizes of clip-on devils' heads. Left, $500-550; Right, $475-525.

Unsilvered pumpkin head. $350-400

Lion head. $500-550

Opposite page:
Assortment of German blown heads. 1st row: $200-225, $160-180, $190-200, $200-210. 2nd row: $90-100, $300-325, $175-200, $80-90. 3rd row: $80-90, $260-285, $300-325, $400-425. 4th row: $300-325, $100-120, $500-525, $190-200. 5th row: $85-95, $135-140, $220-240, $380-400.

Page 118:
Top left: Charlie McCarthy. $400-425
Bottom left: Rare man in moon. $800-900
Top right: Al Jolson. $400-450
Bottom right: Kite face. $400-450
Page 119:
Top left: Bacchus. $500-550
Bottom left: Unsilvered devil. $325-350
Top right: Clown. $140-160
Bottom right: Man smoking cigarette. $950-1100

Lion head in berry cluster. $400-425

Victorian lady bust. $240-260

Two-faced pipe horn. $500-550

Child in daisy blossom. $285-300

Mustached man pipe. $400-425

Clip-on devil. $500-550

President Taft head. $800-900

Sailor head and flower candle holder. $600-700

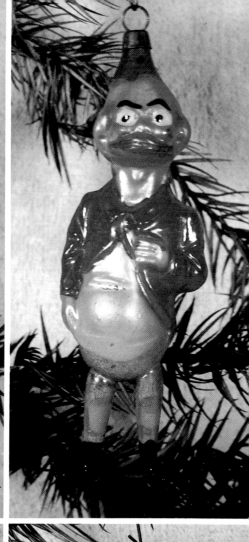

Opposite page:
Top left: Santa with tree head. $300-325
Bottom left: Pincushion angel with wings. $350-400
Top right: Green belsnickle. $500-550
Bottom right: Cigar smoking man, possibly Jigs. $500-600

It is indeed possible that the writer, Kate Greenway, inspired a German craftsman to create these whimsical children's figurals. Notice the exquisite molding of these very early beauties!

Victorian boy with dog. $900-1000

Victorian girl with cat. $900-1000

Page 126:
Top left: Elf with pipe. $160-180
Bottom left: Black boy with accordion. $500-525
Top right: Unsilvered clown with quarter moon. $175-200
Bottom right: Skeezix. $300-325

Page 127:
Top left: Girl in medallioned sack. $400-450
Bottom left: Comic boy figure. $600-650
Top right: Joe E. Lewis (boxer). $250-300
Bottom right: Angel with star. $400-450

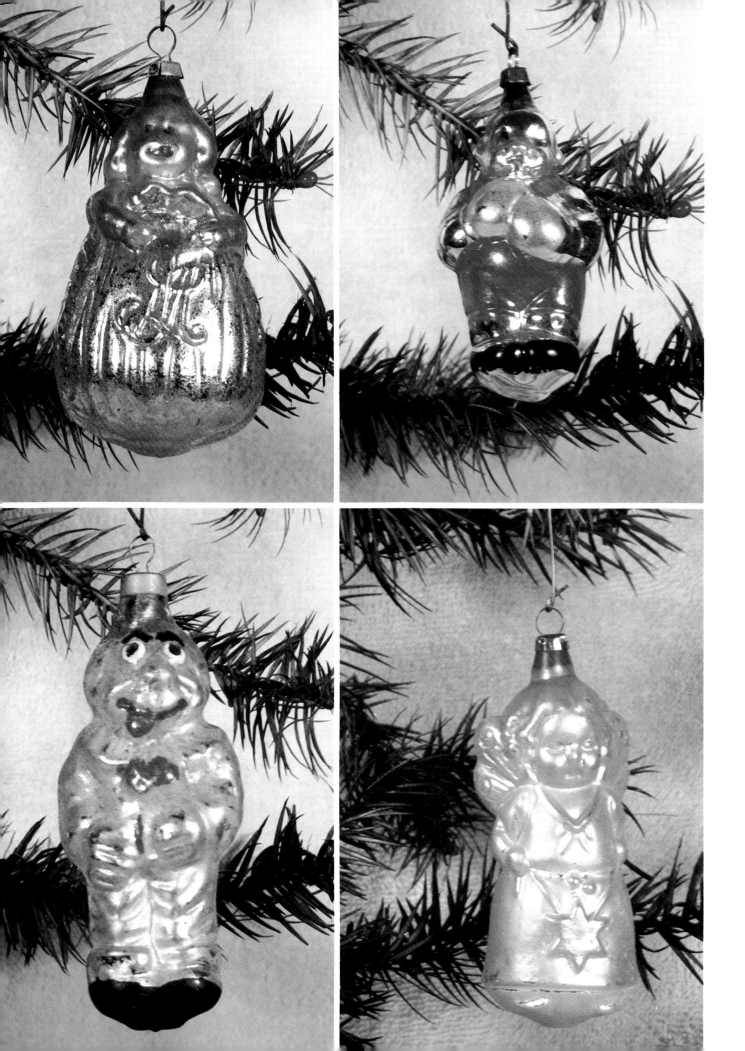

Top left: Clown with chenille limbs. $500-550
Bottom left: Snow Baby girl with tree. $200-225
Top right: Peanut man with chenille limbs. $400-450
Bottom right: Butcher/Baker on clip. $900-1000

Opposite page:
Top left: Pelican. $325-350
Bottom left: Elephant on ball. $400-425
Top right: Seahorse (possibly Italian). $150-160
Bottom right: Monkey with flower. $250-275

Penguin. $200-220

Kitten in shoe. $200-250

Snake with clown head. $300-325

Costumed monkey. $650-700

Four different sizes of elephants. Small to large, $200-250.

Seated bear. $225-250

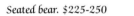

Sitting eagle. $325-350

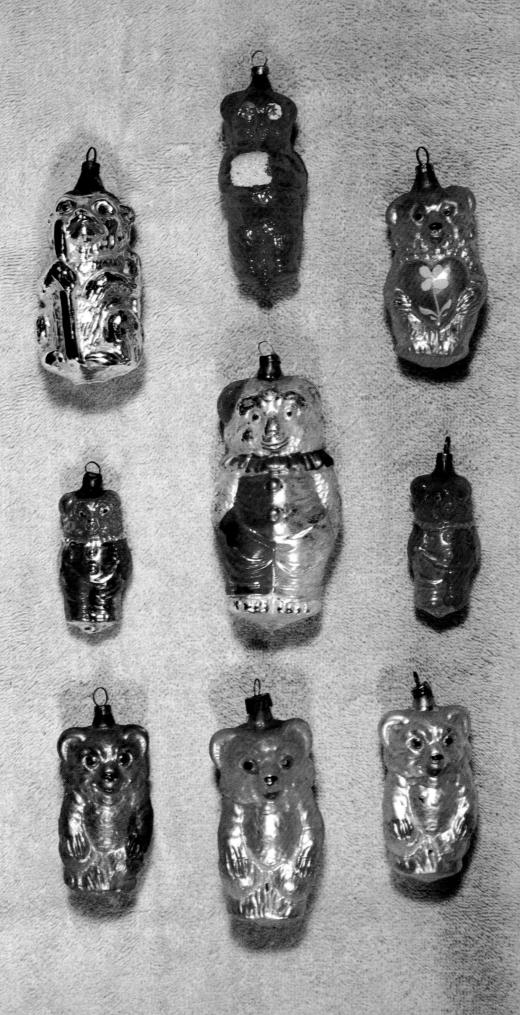

Peacock on clip. $260-280

Owl on clip. $400-450

Turkey on clip. $500-550

Bird on moss nest. $300-325

Opposite page: Different types of bears. Top: $125-140, $135-150, $300-325.
Middle: $90-100, $300-325, $100-125. Bottom: $160-180, $150-210, $140-160.

Considered to be a sign of good luck by our German ancestors, a bird's nest in a Christmas tree has almost been a must for most traditionalists. If Mother Nature can't provide one, collectors can most certainly substitute a glass one. Bird figurals are extremely common, but bird related ornaments, such as nests, are much more rare and more desirable to a collector.

Opposite page:
Top left: Victorian wire-wrapped nest. $400-450
Bottom left: Stork on house. $500-525
Top right: Bird on ball nest. $180-200
Bottom right: Bird in wicker basket nest. $150-170

Bird on log. $400-450

Double birds on nest. $500-550

Single bird on nest. $400-425

Page 136:
Top left: Tree with Santa peeking. $140-160
Bottom left: Silvered baseball. $300-325
Top right: Couple kissing over bush. $275-300
Bottom right: Unsilvered baseball. $250-300

Page 137:
Top left: Stocking with toys. $400-450
Bottom left: Victorian wire-wrapped Victrola. $600-750
Top right: Bowling pin. $120-140
Bottom right: Elaborate indent. $90-100

Early blown daisy. $90-100

Hindenberg air ship. $600-700

Zeppelin air ship. $285-300

Early delicate pipe. $300-325

Opposite pag: Rare clip-on ornaments. Top: $800-850, $600-650, $800-850. Middle: $300-325. Bottom: $400-425, $280-300, $400-450.

Art glass bird's nest, 1930s. $140-160

Art glass elegant deer, 1920s. $140-160

Art glass man with deer, 1920s. $300-325

Art glass fighting roosters, 1920s. $300-325

Opposite page: Delicate blown and indent ornaments. Clockwise: $140-160,
$125-135, $120-140, $145-160, $280-300, $160-175. Middle: $100-125.

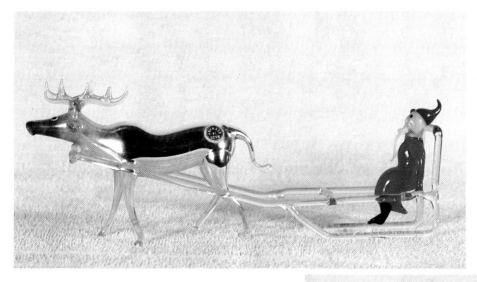

Opposite page:
Top left: Art glass goldfish, 1920s. $125-140
Bottom left; Art glass pipe, 1930s. $160-180
Top right: Art glass cat, 1920s. $175-200
Bottom right: Art glass apple, 1920s. $125-150

Art glass Santa and sleigh, 1920s. $300-325

Art glass fruit, 1930s. $80-90 ea.

Art glass penguin, 1930s. $120-135

Assorted art glass animals, 1930s. $85-100 ea.

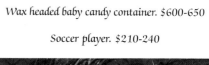

Dog with necktie. $200-225

Wax headed baby candy container. $600-650

Unsilvered rabbit on clip. $500-550

Soccer player. $210-240

Rare chenille limbed figurals. Left to right: $400-450, $500-550, $400-425.

Popcorn head clip-on. $550-600   Andy Gump clip-on. $800-900

Early 1950s Italian figurals. Top: $110-130, $180-200, $95-110. Bottom: $110-130, $100-125, $90-100.

Italian fruit and vegetables, mid-1980s. Top: $50-60, $50-
55. Middle: $140-160. Bottom: $80-90, $55-65.

Fiberboard sailboat, mid-1920s. $125-150

Fiberboard airplane mid-1920s. $140-160

Dresden fish candy container. $500-525

Felix the cat celluloid ornament, 1930s. $650-700

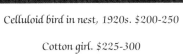

Celluloid bird in nest, 1920s. $200-250

Cotton teddy bear. $365-400

Cotton girl. $225-300

Plaster Father Christmas. $450-500

Dresden figure on glass bell. $800-900

Composition Hitler ornament. $1000-1100

COMBINATION TREE ORNAMENTS.

F3628 — 2 colors wicker basket, asstd. blown glass strawberries, natural colors, moss and leaves. 1 doz. in box............ 25

F3628, 25c Doz.   F3630, 78c Doz.

F3629 — As 3628, larger............ 39

F3630 — *Extra size dime basket.* Neatly woven 2 color basket, 10 pieces asstd. blown glass fruits—apples, oranges, grapes, etc., green leaves. ½ doz. in spaced box.................... 78

Best Selling 5c Asst.
BLOWN GLASS
TREE ORNAMENTS.

Just as popular as ever.

F3639 — Asstd. Brownie figures, well known American characters — policeman, tramp and funny old gent, variety of colors, ht. 5 in. Each with hanger. ½ doz. in spaced box.

Per dozen, **42c**

Butler Brothers, 1905.

Wire candy basket. $145-160

Flat Dresden ornaments. $140-200 ea.

Elaborate flat Dresden ornaments. $150-210 ea.

Rare early 1900s papier-mâché Santa mask with hair. $950-1200

Christmas Crackers, 1930s. $90-110 ea.

Glass Santa container, 1920s. $300-350

Composition boys, Germany U.S. zone. $40-50 ea.

Cast iron nutcracker, early 1900s. $500-550

Plaster groupings, Japan, 1930s. $140-160 ea.

Plaster groupings, Germany, 1930s. $120-140 ea.

Plaster groupings, Germany, 1930s. $85-95 ea.

Large musical wax angel. $800-900

10" Wax angel. $750-850

Feather tree candy container. $175-200

Waxed angel in feather wreath. $400-475

Rare English tin Santa. $900-1000

Composition Santa candy containers, 1930s. $750-900

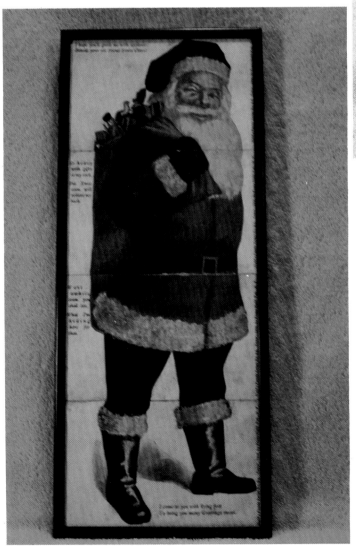

Series of four Santa postcards. $260-300

Rare Sebnitz ornaments before 1900. $325-375 ea.

Early handkerchief. $700-750

Santa stand-up advertising. $250-300 ea.

Above: Champagne advertising stand-up, 1960s. Boot, $100-125; Snowman, $180-200. Below: Santa $450-500.

Ice cream poster, 1940s. $300-350

Large chromolithographed advertising. $500-550

Woven Santa tapestry. $400-425

Santa and sleigh candy container, Japan, 1930s. $190-200

Santa and sleigh container, Japan, 1920s. $200-220

Celluloid Santas from Japan. Left to right: $140-160, $185-200, $260-280.

Santa ceramic mugs, Japan, 1960s. $35-40 ea.

Top: $40-50. Middle: $40-50, $45-60, $80-95, $30-35. Bottom: $35-40.

INDEX—TEXT

Christmas, 1940-1959
A Collector's Guide to Decorations and Customs
Revised 2nd Edition
Robert Brenner

A nostalgic look at Christmas decorating customs, electric lighting innovations, and tree decorations in the USA, featuring machine-produced glass ornaments, bubble lights, Italian miniature lights, Matchless Stars, and many more. Includes historical photos, color photos of decorations from each decade, and detailed text. A treat for collectors, historians, and Christmas enthusiasts.

Size: 8 1/2" x 11"	496 color & 54 b/w photos	160 pp.
Revised Price Guide		
ISBN: 0-7643-1899-3	soft cover	$29.95

Depression Glass for Collectors
Robert Brenner

Originally given as a premium for purchasing certain products during the Depression years, this popular colored table glassware of green, yellow, pink, blue, and other hues is now avidly collected. Pattern names from Adam to Windsor are identified, with a price guide and 360 color photos. This is an important part of glass history and modern culture.

Size: 8 1/2" x 11"	360 color photos	176 pp.
ISBN: 0-7643-0670-7	hard cover	$24.95

Celluloid
Collectibles From the Dawn of Plastics
Robert Brenner

A sweeping survey of the early world of plastics presents celluloid toys, ornaments, jewelry, greeting cards, dolls, and more in over 500 color photographs. Early 20th century catalog copy further chronicles celluloid artifacts and tells a concise and colorful history of celluloid's development (including startling accounts of exploding billiard balls and curling dentures). Values are in the captions and the bibliography leads to further sources.

Size: 8 1/2" x 11"	Over 500 photos	208 pp.
ISBN: 0-7643-0833-5	hard cover	$39.95

Valentine Treasury
A Century of Valentine Cards
Robert Brenner

From the first reference to a valentine card in 1625 to modern times, this book celebrates sentimental charm, wit, and romance over the decades in antique valentines. European origins and American traditions, celebration and card sending customs, card designs and themes, artists and manufacturers from Howland, Whitney, Prang, to Gibson, Hallmark, and American Greetings are included.

Size: 8 1/2" x 11"	565 color photos	208 pp.
ISBN: 0-7643-0195-0	hard cover	$49.95

Christmas Past
Revised 2nd Edition
Robert Brenner

The historical importance, makers, materials, and rarity of Christmas trees, decorations, and ornaments of all kinds are discussed in detail and displayed in color photos, including glass ornaments, all types of lighting from candles to electricity, cotton and paper ornaments, and Dresdens.

Size: 8 1/2" x 11"	250 photos	192 pp.
ISBN: 0-7643-0172-1	soft cover	$29.95

Christmas Through the Decades
With Revised Y2K Prices
Robert Brenner

A chronological illustrated history of how people decorated and celebrated for Christmas. Many antique ornaments from German origins project various customs. Includes newly revised price guide!

Size: 9" x 12"	500 photos	256 pp.
ISBN: 0-88740-545-2	hard cover	$69.95

Christmas 1960 to the Present
A Collector's Guide to Decorations and Customs
Robert Brenner

Innovations and customs in Christmas tree ornaments, lighting, and display of the past 40 years. Interior and exterior lights, artificial trees of the 1960s, candy containers, cards, tinsel garlands, and cheerful holiday figurines used in Christmas celebrations are explained, shown, and valued.

Size: 8 1/2" x 11"	540 color photos	160 pp.
ISBN: 0-7643-1484-X	soft cover	$29.95

Christmas,1940-1959
A Collector's Guide to Decorations and Customs
Robert Brenner

A nostalgic look at Christmas decorating customs, electric lighting innovations, and tree decorations in the U.S., featuring machine-produced glass ornaments, bubble lights, Italian miniature lights, Matchless Stars, and many more. Includes historical photos, color photos of decorations from each decade, and detailed text. A treat for collectors, historians, and Christmas enthusiasts.

Size: 8 1/2" x 11"	496 color &54 b/w photos	160 pp.
ISBN: 0-7643-1475-0	soft cover	$29.95

Christmas Ornaments
A Festive Study
Revised 2nd Edition
Margaret Schiffer

The joy and magic of Christmas are celebrated in this nostalgic pictorial exploration of old-fashioned Christmas decorations. Nearly 1200 enchanting Christmas ornaments, candy containers, Santa figures, and collectibles are displayed in color photos.

Size: 8 1/2" x 11"	262 color plates	168 pp.
ISBN: 0-88740-878-8	soft cover	$29.95

Holidays
Toys and Decorations
Margaret Schiffer

More than 1250 holiday keepsakes shown in color. Begins with New Year's Day, progresses to Valentine's Day, Washington's Birthday, St. Patrick's Day, Easter, Independence Day, Halloween, Thanksgiving, and Christmas. Much to interest the decorators in every home.

Size: 8 1/2" x 11"	253 color photos	144 pp.
ISBN: 0-88740-038-8	soft cover	$19.95

Christmas Tree Pins
O Christmas Tree
Nancy Yunker Trowbridge

Over 1100 different Christmas tree pins, from the mid-20th century to the present, made by more than 200 designers and manufacturers. More than 1,200 color photographs are presented and the pins are described, identified, and valued. The rhinestones, enamels, and metalwork are of the finest quality. Collectors enjoy finding Christmas tree pins all year long.

Size: 8 1/2" x 11"	1200+ color photos	192 pp.
ISBN: 0-7643-1656-7	soft cover	$29.95

Christmas Jewelry
Revised 2nd Edition
Mary Morrison with photographs by James Morrison

Over 340 dazzling photographs of over 900 Christmas tree pins and wreaths, snowmen, Santas and ornaments of costume jewelry. Ranging in price from a few dollars to hundreds, this jewelry is growing in popularity because it delights all. Text includes company histories and revised Price Guide.

Size: 9" x 6"	343 photos	160 pp.
ISBN: 0-7643-1531-5	soft cover	$19.95

A Ron Ransom Christmas
Ron Ransom

With this book anyone can learn to carve the traditional holiday figure using simple hand tools. Step-by-step carving and painting techniques described in full, with tips on "antiquing," and hints on how to make small improvisations on the projects to make them all unique. Included are a torch-bearing "Olympic" Santa, a Santa on skis, and a Santa with snowman. A color gallery shows the finished results in detail.

Size: 8 1/2" X 11"	250 photos	64 pp.
ISBN: 0-7643-0361-9	soft cover	$14.95

Making Christmas Jewelry in Polymer Clay
Bridget Albano

Spread Christmas cheer with festive necklaces, pins and earrings of your own making. Patterns for endearing angels, Christmas trees, gifts, holly, gingerbread men, teddy bears, and old Saint Nick himself are provided, with easily followed instructions and clear color photography. With a few simple tools, everyone—from the youngest to the oldest — will enjoy this book.

Size: 8 1/2" x 11"	208 color photos, 14 patterns	64 pp.
ISBN: 0-88740-832-X	soft cover	$12.95

Holiday Plastic Novelties: The Styrene Toys
Charlene Pinkerton

Styrene plastic novelties flourished in the 1930s and 1940s. Cheap and cheerful, styrene toys, decorations, and party favors brought bright color to holiday celebrations. This book is packed with more than 600 color photos, a price guide, and interesting information.

Size: 8 1/2" x 11"	over 600 color photos	160 pp.
ISBN: 0-7643-0781-9	soft cover	$24.95

30 Holiday Patterns for Carvers
Al Streetman

Here are 30 patterns for holidays throughout the year that feature the creativity and guidance of Al Streetman. These carvings are simple enough to inspire confidence in the beginner and clever enough to allow for a lot of creativity from the experienced carver. In his easygoing manner, Al offers plenty of tips for technique and presentation.

Size: 8 1/2" x 11"	106 color photos, 48 illustrations	64 pp.
ISBN: 0-7643-0514-X	soft cover	$14.95

Country and Folk Antiques
Don and Carol Raycraft

Gathered from Maine to California by veteran folk art enthusiasts, these antiques of country origin include kitchen furnishings, stoneware, baskets, toys, garden ornaments and even Christmas decorations. So many examples are included that it is easy to compare the items through over 500 color photos and the Price Guide. The book is informative and fun.

Size: 8 1/2" x 11"   over 540 color photos   176 pp.
ISBN: 0-88740-828-1   soft cover $29.95

The Encyclopedia of Head Vases
Kathleen Cole

Head vases of many styles are discussed, especially those not seen in print before. 976 color photographs, identifying size, and marks of 1309 heads make identification easy. Special chapters cover popular Betty Lou Nichols heads, Christmas heads, wall pockets, and related collectibles.

Size: 8 1/2" x 11"   976 color photos   208 pp.
ISBN: 0-88740-928-8   hard cover $29.95

Nativity
Créches of the World
Leslie Piña & Lorita Winfield

This book showcases a wide variety of Nativity sets that display multi-cultural artistic interpretations of the true meaning of Christmas. Artisans from more than forty countries on five continents are represented, each with beautiful expressions of the greatest story ever told, often with photographs from the country of origin to accompany the artwork. Whether sculpted in clay, carved from wood, painted, woven, or cast, these Cre*ches from around the world are sure to enhance holiday celebrations and illustrate the universality of the Christmas message.

Size: 8 1/2" x 11"   537 color photos   144 pp.
ISBN: 0-7643-1212-X   hard cover $29.95

Angel Collectibles
Debra S. Braun

Angels have inspired great art and countless pieces of memorabilia. This book contains antique to modern angel collectibles (i.e., statues, perfume bottles, Christmas decorations, etc.) Some of the manufacturers included are: Dreamsicles™, Hallmark™, Hummel™ Lladro™ Kewpie™, and Precious Moments™. Nearly 400 color photos, descriptions, and price guide.

Size: 8 1/2" x 11"   394 color photos   160 pp.
ISBN: 0-7643-1342-8   soft cover $29.95

Schiffer books may be ordered from your local bookstore, or they may be ordered directly from the publisher by writing to:
Schiffer Publishing, Ltd.
4880 Lower Valley Rd
Atglen PA 19310
(610) 593-1777; Fax (610) 593-2002
E-mail: Info@schifferbooks.com
Please visit our website catalog at **www.schifferbooks.com** or write for a free catalog. Please include $3.95 for shipping and handling for the first two books and $1.00 for each additional book. Free shipping for orders of $100 or more.
Printed in China